INTO THE LABYRINTH

An Anatomy of Position Playing for Jazz Guitar

DAVY MOONEY

Online Audio

To access the online audio recording go to:
WWW.MELBAY.COM/31070MEB

WWW.MELBAY.COM

CONTENTS

CHAPTER 1

Introduction to the Labyrinth

Fluency Over Tunes

I had just performed John Coltrane's "26-2," a highly intricate harmonic puzzle. I sat down to my laptop to take questions from the University of North Texas Jazz Guitar department via Zoom (this was during the height of Covid-isolation). The opening query via the chat window was this: "Talk about how you develop fluency over tunes."

If jazz is a language, then it is fluency we seek. I began to mentally reverse-engineer the process by which I arrived at a reasonable command of the fretboard. It has been a long journey, and looking back I picked things up in bits and pieces, in scraps of knowledge. There was no grand design or recognizable system that I followed; I put smaller parts of various systems to use for my own particular artistic ends.

At UNT I have been blessed with students who play at an incredibly high level. In many cases, fretboard knowledge and questions of patterns, shapes, and scales don't come up because these players are fluent already. If anything, I teach them from my experience—years of hustling, playing gigs, and writing and making records. But I have come to realize that *my* journey through the maze of the fretboard is worth describing in detail, in case others wish to follow.

The Labyrinth

The guitar fretboard is a labyrinth ruled by shapes and patterns. It has its own logic, actuated by the standard-tuning system of perfect 4th intervals between each string except the third and second, which are separated by a major 3rd. There is nothing intuitive about it, unlike the piano, with its regular recurrence of white and black keys in each octave. Every area of the guitar fretboard has its twists and turns.

Most guitarists begin by learning "cowboy chords"—voicings using open strings—which enable one to play much of the rock and folk repertoire of American popular music. Likewise, many beginning guitar method books, such as Mel Bay, Alfred, Hal Leonard, and others, start by teaching the C major scale in the open position.

Strumming "Wish You Were Here" and "Hotel California," or sight-reading "Camptown Races"—these are all fine and good, but when a guitarist wishes to move into the realm of improvised music and jazz, a deeper knowledge of the fretboard is required, and some system, some method to traverse this mysterious labyrinth must be learned.

Five Major Scale Shapes

I'd like to narrate my own journey through the labyrinth, from a 9-year-old strumming the aforementioned classic rock standards, to a budding jazz player improvising on "So What" and "Little Sunflower" at Loyola Jazz Camp in the summer of 1993. There was no internet back then, and what information I received was from actual human beings—teachers, uncles, friends—and it came in the form of sheets of paper, physically handed to me, or contained in guitar magazines I picked up at the grocery store while shopping with my parents.

I went to several summer jazz camps in my early adolescence, and was usually placed in an intermediate combo, because I had a natural facility on the instrument and a command of the blues scale, a handful of jazz-adjacent barre chords, and probably one form of the major scale. In 1993 I was given a sheet of paper with a printout of the five shapes of the major scale that I later learned represented the "CAGED" system. I don't remember relating the five shapes to any open chord forms or anything like that, and the document is long lost, but I remember vividly that I went home that evening and sat in my room for two hours, memorizing the fingerings of these five shapes:

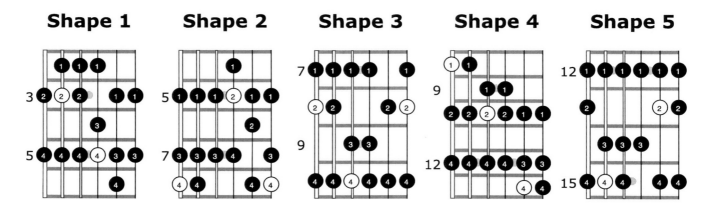

Example 1

For those of you who are new to fretboard diagrams such as these, the numbers on the left, outside of the diagrams, are the fret numbers. The numbers inside the dark circles are the left-hand finger numbers; the white circles are the root notes of the scales and arpeggios. The orientation is vertical, so just imagine a guitar hanging on a wall, or visualize a headstock at the top of each image.

The reader might see these shapes and fingerings and think "That's not the CAGED system I learned! What is that weird fourth shape with three notes per string?" *We all have to navigate the labyrinth on our own. What I am describing here is **my** journey.*

The above diagrams contain the five shapes in C major, in various areas of the fretboard, but the notation below indicates the same five shapes *in the same area of the fretboard*, to demonstrate how important it was for me to at first memorize the *fingerings*, rather than the *appearance* of each shape in a specific area of the fretboard. As we will see in later chapters, when you try to stay in one area of the fretboard while playing a song that modulates frequently, muscle memory is very important, for both scale shapes and arpeggios. In my case memorizing fingerings was the first step toward muscle memorization.

I am also deliberately avoiding tablature, instead using a system of fingerings that I learned from the fabulous Barry Galbraith books, wherein the circled number below the staff represents the string while the un-circled numbers refer to the left-hand fingers. I have nothing against tablature, but any opportunity I can take to try to get guitar players to deal with written music and be better readers is one I must seize!

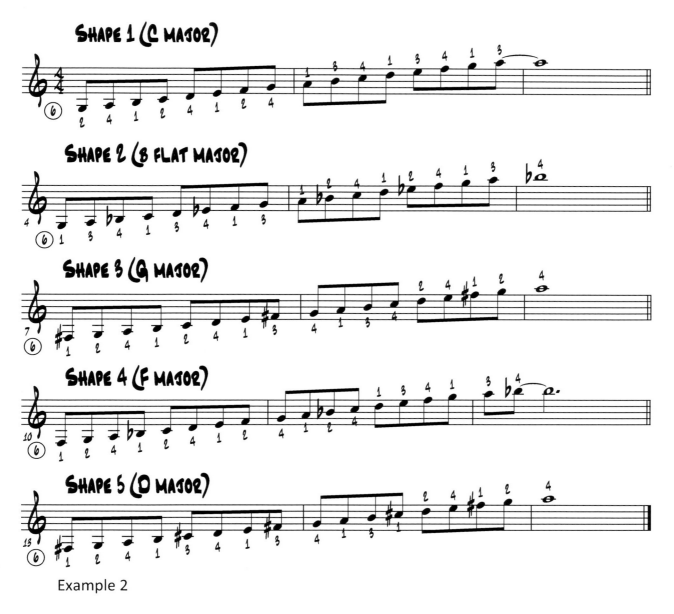

Example 2

Learning these five shapes, this modified CAGED system that came to me via hard copy in the summer of 1993, allowed me to return to camp the next day and improvise over "So What," "Little Sunflower," and other modal tunes over the entire guitar fretboard. This was the first faint illumination of a path through the labyrinth, although it would take years for me to feel comfortable and fluent improvising over jazz tunes, especially those with frequent modulations.

Arpeggio Shapes

I began jazz guitar lessons in earnest sometime the next year with the great teacher and player, the guru of New Orleans jazz guitar, Hank Mackie. I remember going through tunes like "Lady Bird" and "Lucky Southern" with Hank, mapping out the major scale key areas of the progressions so I could apply my scale-shape knowledge on a repertoire beyond modal jazz. I discovered very quickly that, while I was able to play in the right keys and not hit obvious wrong notes (nailing down what *right* and *wrong* notes are in jazz is always fraught), my improvising didn't sound much like the classic jazz that I was beginning to listen to, like Wes Montgomery on *A Dynamic New Sound*. In my previous book, *Personalizing Jazz Vocabulary* (MB30786M), I describe the method by which I began to apply classic jazz phrases to my improvising, but I didn't say much about the actual *improvised* part of my playing. One needs a collection of licks and tropes to begin to access the jazz language, but it is also a good idea to try to hear melodies and play them in real time—to cultivate what Joe Pass called in his 1970 book *Joe Pass Guitar Style* the "ear/hand relationship"—and I found that scales were less effective than arpeggios in getting to the melodies I was beginning to hear.

Fortunately, Hank showed me some arpeggio shapes, which I still use, that enabled me to connect the five shapes of the major scale across the length of the fretboard. From now on I'll refer to the ascending and descending of the frets from 1 to 21 as the *length* of the fretboard, and the ascending and descending of the strings from 6 to 1 as the *width* of the fretboard. We'll forget about height for now, our labyrinth has only two dimensions.

I remember learning these shapes on three sets of strings: 3, 2, 1; 4, 3, 2; and 5, 4, 3. The arpeggios represent the diatonic seventh chords that occur in every major key: I Ma7, ii mi7, iii mi7, IV Ma7, V 7, vi mi7, vii mi7♭5. I used to practice these with the following fingerings, usually beginning with the lowest arpeggio that occurs on the length of the fretboard on each string set. I would play around with different patterns as well, for instance ascending the Bmi7♭5 arpeggio in Example 3 below to the A natural on the first string, then shifting up to the B natural two frets higher and descending the CMa7 arpeggio that follows. I would also practice different note values, including triplets and sixteenths. Here are the shapes in the key of C, in both fretboard diagrams and standard notation:

Strings 3, 2, 1

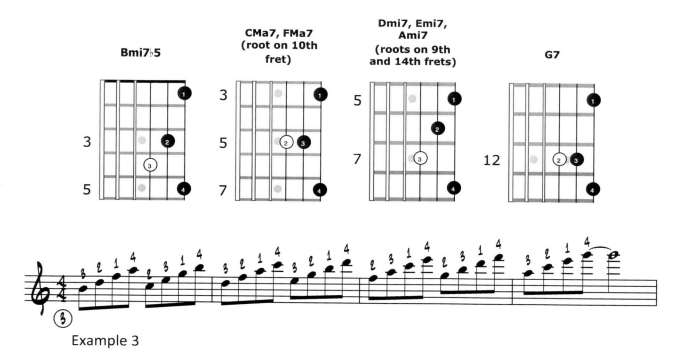

Example 3

Strings 4, 3, 2

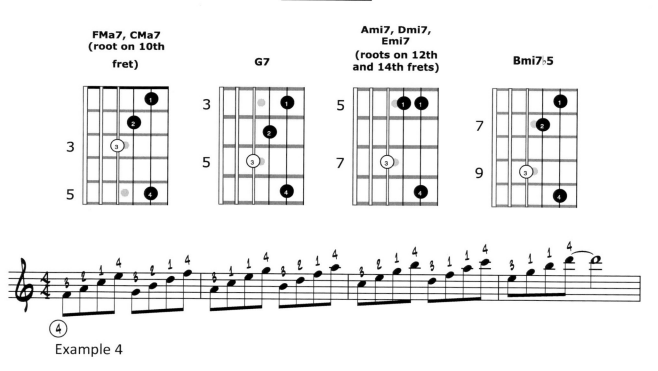

Example 4

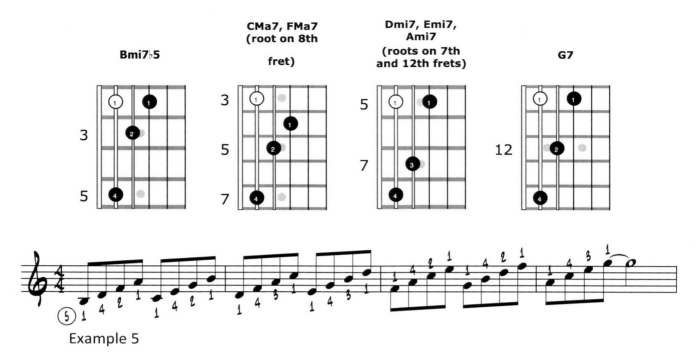

Example 5

There are of course other ways to finger these arpeggios, and I am not arguing that these fingerings are the best or even the most efficient, but they were the ones that I used to learn the fretboard. As we will see later on, I have more specific shapes that I currently use to improvise over tunes.

In conjunction with these arpeggios, I remember Hank asking me to get a notebook wherein he wrote out the chord spellings for Ma7, 7, mi7, and mi7♭5. We took these chords through their upper extensions, and I remember I had a chart that looked something like this:

	R	3	5	7	9	11	13
CMa7	C	E	G	B	D	F (or F♯)	A
C7	C	E	G	B♭	D	F (or F♯)	A
Cmi7	C	E♭	G	B♭	D	F	A
Cmi7♭5	C	E♭	G♭	B♭	D♭ (or D)	F	A♭

Example 6

From this chart I could glean that a CMa7 arpeggio from the third was Emi7, a Cmi7 from the third was E♭Ma7, a C7 from the third was Emi7♭5, a Cmi7♭5 from the third was E♭mi7, and all manner of other mysteries.

Armed with this new knowledge, my diatonic improvising became more chord-specific, and I was able to access the upper extensions of the chords, so important to improvising in a modern jazz style. As Ralph Ellison quotes Charlie Parker in his superb essay *On Bird, Bird-Watching, and Jazz*:

I remember one night before Monroe's I was jamming in a chili house on Seventh Avenue between 139th and 140th. It was December, 1939…I'd been getting bored with the stereotyped changes that were being used all the time, all the time, and I kept thinking there's bound to be something else. I could hear it sometimes but I couldn't play it. Well, that night, I was working over "Cherokee," and, as I did, I found that by using the higher intervals of a chord as a melody line and backing them with appropriately related changes, I could play the thing I'd been hearing. I came alive.

The labyrinth was now glowing with potentiality. I had my major scales and understood how to apply them modally on standard jazz progressions. I had the arpeggio shapes that allowed me to connect the CAGED system, lengthwise. And I had learned that when I played an Emi7 arpeggio it would also work on a CMa7, or even an FMa7#11 (and more revelations were to come on this front). I mixed all this up with ii-V-I licks, and fragments of the jazz language picked up from Hank, Steve Masakowski, Clyde Kerr, Jr. at NOCCA, records of Wes Montgomery, Joe Pass, Tal Farlow, Barney Kessel, Jimmy Raney, and many others. It was a slow process, but I was making steady progress in becoming fluent in the jazz language and on the fretboard of the guitar.

Improvising In All-8th Notes

Another important step in my development, and the third leg of the stool that supports the content of this book, was the practice of improvising in all-8th notes over standards, at slow tempos with metronome only, trying to confine myself to specific areas of the fretboard and attempting to make a very technical, etude-like exercise sound as musical as possible. I must once again tip my hat to Barry Galbraith, whose books *The Fretboard Workout* and *Melodic and Harmonic Minor Modes* contain perhaps the finest all-8th note studies in jazz guitar literature.

Through the daily practice of improvising in all-8ths on standards, I began to play longer lines, and to connect ideas chromatically. Indeed, I developed a sort of muscle memory that helped my fingers know how many 8ths were needed to get from point A to point B, from one consonant arpeggio note to the next. It was through this process that I began to formulate the concept of *five and nine eighth-note resolution cells* that I wrote about in my previous book *Personalizing Jazz Vocabulary* (MB30786M), and which I will refer to in later chapters of this book.

So the three essential elements that led to my eventual fluency on the fretboard of the guitar were **my knowledge of scale shapes** (major at first, but later melodic and harmonic minor, harmonic major, and various pentatonics), **my linking of those scale shapes with ascending arpeggios on string sets 1-3, 2-4, and 3-5** (and later other combinations and fingerings), **and my diligent practice of playing all-8th notes on standards, trying to be as musical as possible**.

Now of course I teach and run the jazz guitar program at UNT, where the level of playing is very high. Some students come to me already fluent on the fretboard of the guitar, and they have learned different systems than the CAGED shapes I was handed back in 1993. They can watch countless instructional videos on YouTube and scour the internet for scale and arpeggio shapes and patterns. They can even watch live footage of their favorite players, with closeups of their hands! If students come to me already fluent on the fretboard, we don't spend time on scale or arpeggio shapes. If they can play long, interesting lines and phrase well in a classic jazz style, we don't practice playing all-8th notes in positions over standards.

But if I'm working with a student who is only comfortable in certain parts of the fretboard, or who seems to always arpeggiate chords from the root, or who can only improvise short phrases—I take them through my own process of achieving fretboard fluency.

What This Book Contains

In the five chapters that follow in this book, I take five standard jazz progressions and demonstrate how I improvise over them on the fretboard of the guitar, in five general areas, roughly corresponding to the modified CAGED system I learned all those years ago. I have composed five one-chorus, all-8th note etudes on each progression, one for each area of the fretboard. These studies are followed by five one-chorus improvisations in the same sequence— one chorus on each chunk of the fretboard, ascending. **Following each etude and improvisation I break the progressions down into smaller sections and provide fretboard diagrams for each section that show the specific shapes I used to compose the etudes and to improvise.** These shapes recur again and again, transposed to different areas of the fretboard. Over the years, my scale and arpeggio shapes have become more specific and specialized as I have discovered what works best for me as a player, but they all come from the scale shapes I learned at Loyola jazz camp in 1993 and the arpeggio shapes Hank showed me shortly thereafter.

There are downloadable recordings of me performing each etude and improvisation, along with backing tracks of both solo guitar (for you to practice your own all-8th note playing), and guitar, bass, and drums (for you to practice improvising in positions). There are 60 recordings in all. Joining me in the rhythm section are the fabulous Dallas-Fort Worth-based musicians drummer Matt Young (who also engineered the recording) and bassist Mike Luzecky.

The system that I have devised to navigate through the labyrinth of the guitar fretboard (and the daunting labyrinth of jazz harmony) always seemed to me to be composed of fragments of information that I picked up from diverse sources over the years, but when I stop to explain what I am doing I realize that it is very specific. There are shapes and figurations that I use over and over—although I use them to improvise, so the sequence of ideas, shapes, and patterns is never identical.

So read on, and enter yet another labyrinth: that of my mind, as it tries to make sense of both the fretboard of the guitar and the complicated harmonic puzzles that make up modern jazz.

CHAPTER 2

Miles-Type Changes

The chord changes that provide the harmonic framework for this chapter's all-8th note etudes and improvisations modulate four times, from C minor to F Major, E♭ Major, and D♭ Major. The chord progression itself consists of: minor 6th and 7th chords, dominant 7th chords, major 6th chords, and one minor 7♭5 chord.

As I explain in *Personalizing Jazz Vocabulary* (MB30786M), under the influence of Barry Harris and his "6th Diminished Scale" I have taken to notating and conceptualizing the tonic chord in major and minor keys as a 6th chord rather than a major or minor 7th. The minor mode is more complicated as there are several forms, and an argument could be made that the i chord in a minor key is a minor-major 7th or perhaps even a simple minor triad, but a lengthy dive into this subject is beyond the scope of this book. If this use of 6ths instead of 7ths seems strange to you, please chalk it up to my personal idiosyncrasies and add it to the list!

For each of these chord types, in each area of the fretboard, I have specific shapes that I use to improvise. These shapes include scale patterns related to the CAGED system I learned back in 1993 (Chapter 1, Example 1), as well as arpeggio shapes derived from those I introduced in Chapter 1, Examples 3-5.

Let's begin with the first area of the fretboard, covering roughly frets 2 to 6. I conceptualize this five-fret area as Position 1 because it is the lowest chunk of the fretboard where I can improvise on all the chords of this progression without using open strings (although of course there's nothing wrong with open strings).

On the following page you will find the all-8th note etude I composed and the chorus I improvised in this position.

MILES-TYPE CHANGES ETUDE #1

MILES-TYPE CHANGES IMPROV #1

The fingerings provided are the ones I use, but feel free to use your own if you find them awkward. Over the first chord, the Cmi6, I'm using a combination of arpeggios and the C harmonic minor scale over both the etude and improvisation, which I play in this position using these shapes:

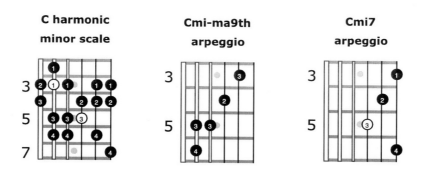

Example 7

(Remember that for all these fretboard diagrams the general idea is to start with the lowest-sounding note and ascend, although the goal is to use them to improvise. Once they enter muscle-memory you can start where you like).

Notice that for the Cmi-ma7th arpeggio I start on the 2nd degree of the scale rather than the root. In this etude and improvisation I don't use the Cmi7 arpeggio, but when improvising at length I use it often. As I stated in Chapter 1, the minor mode is tricky because you can vary the 6th and 7th degrees of the scale. Sometimes I make the i chord Dorian, sometimes harmonic or melodic minor. I may use all of these sounds over the course of a longer improvisation.

I will analyze the following ii-V-I progression, Gmi7-C7-F6, as a unit. The progression is in the key of F, so I use the F major scale to improvise. I also have arpeggio shapes that I use for each of the three chords, as well as some altered language for the dominant. On this C7 I actually improvise the same thing that I composed for the etude, and part of me wanted to change one or the other, but keeping them the same illustrates an important point: **I use the same shapes and figurations again and again, and that doesn't make me less of an improviser.** For more thoughts on this subject I recommend the Chick Corea article, "The Myth of Improvisation," from an old issue of the now-defunct *Keyboard* magazine. Here are the shapes:

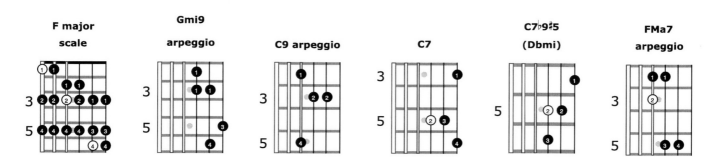

Example 8

Notice again that on the Gmi9 and C9 arpeggios I am starting on either the 3rd or a half step below the 3rd. You could also think of these arpeggios as BbMa7 and Emi7b5. The C7b9♯5 shape that I use in this position is also a Dbmi shape. Remember that on a dominant 7th chord resolving V-I you can play a minor sound up a half step; the fabled Super Locrian mode of melodic minor is one way to conceptualize this. There is also a C augmented triad within the shape. The next progression is another ii-V, this time in the key of Eb. Here are the shapes:

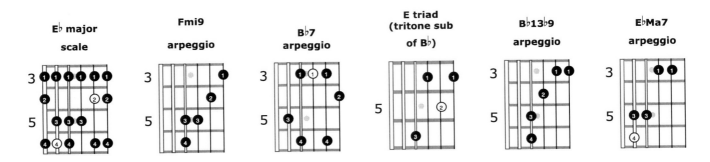

Example 9

Again, the Fmi9 is also an AbMa7; the Bb9 is a Dmi7b5. I alter the Bb7 in the etude with a half-whole diminished 13b9 sound, incorporating a G triad over the Bb7, while in the improvisation I use an E triad, the tritone sub of Bb. Here are the shapes for the next ii-V:

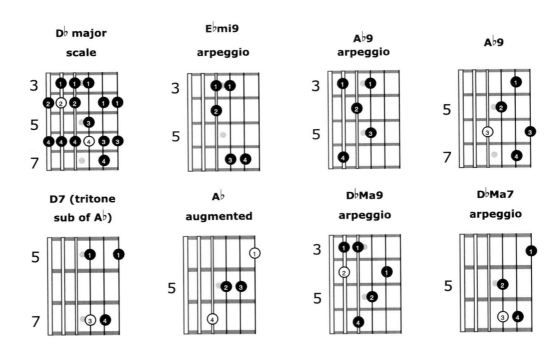

Example 10

In the improvisation, the ii-V bar contains mostly rests. Music needs to breathe, and this was a logical place to do so. The shapes above are what *I would* use to improvise over these chords in this part of the fretboard. Once again, the ii and V chords are conceptualized from the third. On the A♭7 I have provided shapes for an augmented triad and a tritone substitution, although I only use the augmented sound in the etude. **Augmented triads sound very elegant on dominant 7th chords—I get a lot of mileage out of them.** Sometimes I also play a multi-octave, multi-position augmented arpeggio like this:

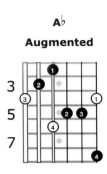

A♭

Augmented

Example 11

The final cadence in this progression is Dmi7♭5 to G7, resolving back to Cmin at the top of the chorus. In the improvisation I use the C harmonic minor scale from Example 7 over ii and V, while in the etude I use a pentatonic collection derived from the G half-whole diminished scale, with the pitches B, D♭, D, F, and G outlining a G7♭5 chord. Here are the shapes for G half-whole diminished and the G7♭5 pentatonic. For C harmonic minor refer back to Example 7:

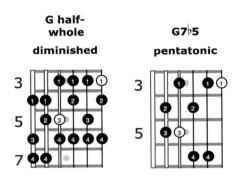

G half-whole diminished

G7♭5 pentatonic

Example 12

The second area of the fretboard encompasses frets 5 to 9, more or less. The all-8th note etude and the improvised chorus are on the following page.

MILES-TYPE CHANGES ETUDE #2

MILES-TYPE CHANGES IMPROV #2

Over the Cmi6 in this position I use the following shapes:

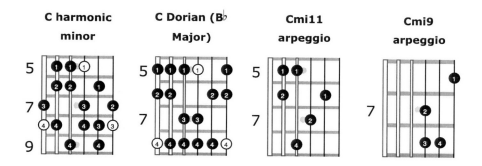

Example 13

I also sometimes combine the two Cmi9 arpeggios into this two-octave arpeggio, which extends up to the 10th fret:

Example 14

This line could also work over EbMa7, F7sus, and Ami7b5, due to the commonality of the chord tones. Here are the shapes for the ii-V in F in this position:

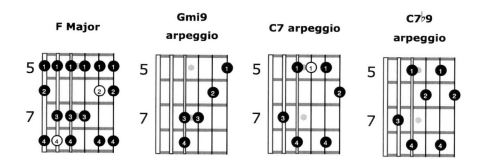

Example 15

Notice that these shapes are basically the same as those in Example 9, although the key is different. **This is in some ways the point of this book. The shapes that I use are the same in every part of the fretboard—only the frets and key centers change.** Read on for the ii-V in Eb in this position.

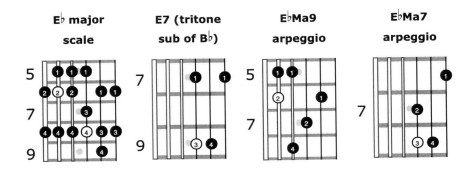

Example 16

These are the specific shapes I use in this etude and improvisation, but I could have used any of the shapes from Example 10, transposed to this key (shifted up 2 frets). Likewise, the two-octave arpeggio in Example 14 that I use over Cmi6 could also be used over Eb6 here. Here are the shapes for the ii-V in Db:

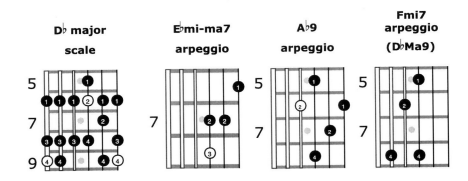

Example 17

The language I use over the ii-V in this position is highly chromatic, and **I encourage you to study all these etudes and improvisations for their purely musical value, beyond the shapes and fingerings.** This Ab9 arpeggio wasn't used in this case, although it is a shape I often employ. Once again, the DbMa9 arpeggio is conceived of as an Fmi7, because DbMa7 from the 3rd *is* Fmi7 (see Example 6, Chapter 1). Here are the shapes for the last ii-V:

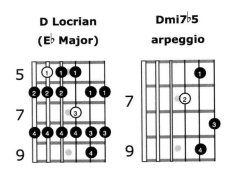

Example 18

The D Locrian shape is identical to the E♭ major scale shape in Example 16, and I also use the C harmonic minor scale from Example 13 in both the etude and the improvisation.

Here are the etude and improvisation in the next position:

MILES-TYPE CHANGES ETUDE #3

MILES-TYPE CHANGES IMPROV #3

The third area of the fretboard spans frets 7 to 12. The Cmi9 arpeggio in this position is similar to the Gmi7 in Example 8, Position 1, although this arpeggio is ornamented by notes culled from the C harmonic minor scale instead of the Dorian mode:

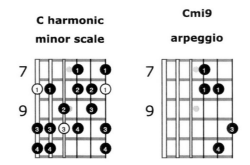

Example 19

Here is a two-octave arpeggio (similar to Example 14) that I often play in this position, although it didn't make it into the etude or the improvisation:

Example 20

This line would also work over F7#11, B7alt, EbMa7#5, and Ami9b5, similar to Example 14.

The ii-V in F in this position is just like the ii-V in Eb in Position 2 and the ii-V in Db in Position 1. In the improvisation I alter the C7 by superimposing an A triad, lending a 13b9, diminished flavor to the passage:

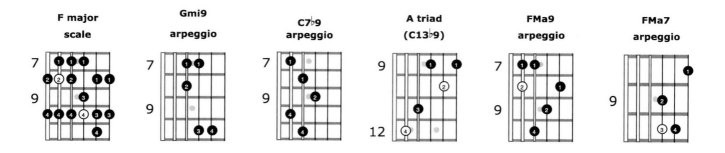

Example 21

The language in both the etude and the improvisation is highly chromatic, and **there is an instance of over-the-barline phrasing in measures 4-5 as the C13b9 is extended one beat into**

the F6. I use this technique often. The ii-V in E♭ in this position is like the ii-V in D♭ in Position 2, and some of these shapes are the same as those in Example 17:

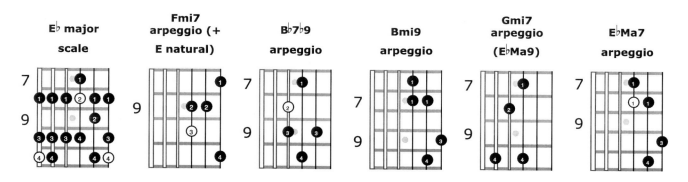

Example 22

The language in measures 7-9 of the etude is highly chromatic, but these are the shapes from which the chromaticism is derived. **Without a substructure of strong chord tones to ornament, I would just be playing the chromatic scale. All my chromaticism is ornamentation of arpeggios and scale fragments.** There is also an interesting harmonic maneuver in measure 8 of the improvisation where I superimpose a Bmi9 arpeggio over the B♭7. I explain this technique in some detail in *Personalizing Jazz Vocabulary* (MB30786M), specifically in Example 21, page 24, but the general idea is that I am using the tritone sub of the ii chord, Fmi7, instead of the V, which would be an E major triad. You can hear this technique in the playing of Bud Powell, Wes Montgomery, and others. The ii-V in D♭ in this position uses some shapes we haven't yet encountered:

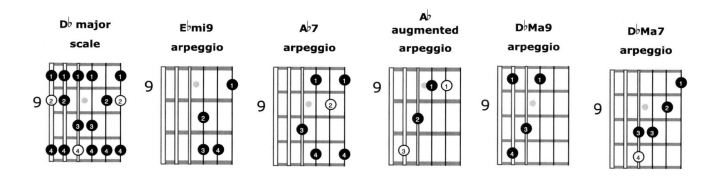

Example 23

As I stated after Example 10, **I think augmented triads are a very elegant way to alter dominants. They are also very versatile and sound good in varied contexts, including bebop, traditional jazz, and modern jazz.** In the improvisation, I extend the A♭ augmented triad into the D♭6 bar, another example of over-the-barline playing.

21

The notes I play in measure 11 of the etude are a figuration I use frequently. I first learned this two-octave arpeggio from Steve Masakowski, and it also appears at the end of Joe Pass's solo on "Meditation" from the 1969 recording *Intercontinental* (at about 3:25 in the recording I have):

Example 24

For the final minor ii-V in this position, I'm using the harmonic minor scale from Example 19, which itself contains a G augmented triad. You can finger it like the one in Example 23, page 21, but don't forget to move down a half-step. The notes in measures 12-13 of both the etude and the improvisation are great examples of five and nine eighth-note resolution cells. For a deep dive into this topic, see Chapter 2 of *Personalizing Jazz Vocabulary* (MB30786M).

The fourth etude and improvisation are on the following page.

MILES-TYPE CHANGES ETUDE #4

MILES-TYPE CHANGES IMPROV #4

The fourth area of the fretboard consists of frets 10 to 14 or so. Once again, for Cmi6 in this position the C harmonic minor scale is essential, and in both choruses above I combine C harmonic minor with C Dorian and the G♭ "blues note."

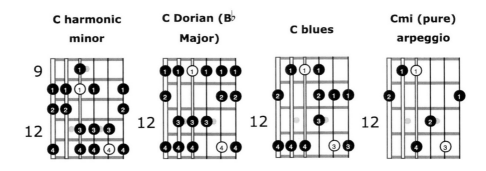

Example 25

In this position, the ii-V in F is similar to the ii-Vs in E♭ in Position 3 and D♭ in Position 2:

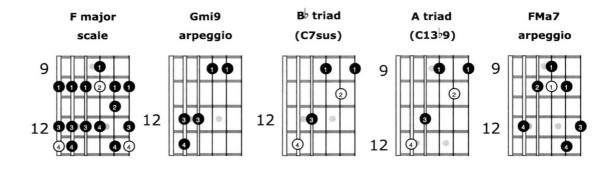

Example 26

The language on the C7 in the etude and improvisation is highly chromatic, but based on the C Mixolydian scale, along with a descent from a B♭ triad to an A triad. This movement evokes a C7sus to a C13♭9 sound. Also, over the F6 there is idiomatic chromaticism. **If you want to sound like you're playing bebop, or what I call *classic jazz*, this is the type of vocabulary you need.** The ii-V in E♭ in this position is like the ii-V in D♭ in Position 3 (Example 23):

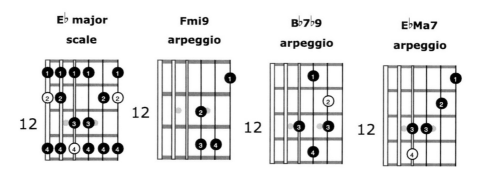

Example 27

There is chromaticism in this ii-V as well, and an over-the-barline, delayed resolution to the E♭6 in measure 9—the B♭7♭9 material extends one beat into the E♭6. The ii-V in D♭ in this position harkens back to the ii-V in F in Position 1 and the shapes in Example 8:

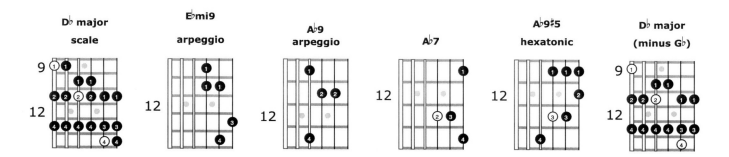

Example 28

I don't use all of these shapes in this position's etude and improvisation, but in a longer improvisation they would come in handy. The line in measure 10 of the etude uses the above A♭9♯5 shape in a five eighth-note resolution cell that I play often, made up of the four eighth-notes on beats 3 and 4 of measure 10, resolving to the A♭ on the downbeat of measure 11. I find the ♯5, ♮9 combination to be very musical, and reminiscent of players such as Wes Montgomery and Joe Pass. I also often use the D♭ major scale without the perfect 4th interval. **These days I often end up with six-note, hexatonic collections, and I'm not sure if I'm playing major scales with one note subtracted or pentatonic scales with one note added!**

The last ii-V uses C harmonic minor in the improvisation while in the etude there is an interesting movement from an A♭Ma7 to a G triad with an added ♯5, using these shapes:

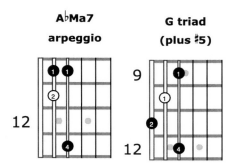

Example 29

The etude and improvisation for the final position are on the following page.

MILES-TYPE CHANGES ETUDE #5

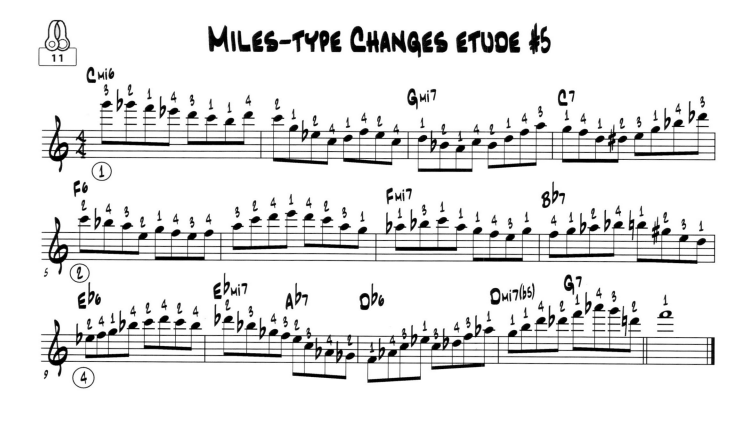

MILES-TYPE CHANGES IMPROV #5

This last position encompasses frets 12 to 16, more or less. For the Cmi6, I am mostly using harmonic minor with some chromaticism, but the mi9 arpeggio in the following example (which we've seen several times already) is also useful.

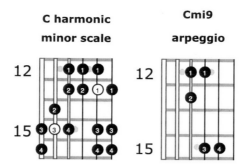

C harmonic minor scale

Cmi9 arpeggio

Example 30

The ii-V in F in this position resembles the ii-V in E♭ in Position 4 and the ii-V in D♭ in Position 3:

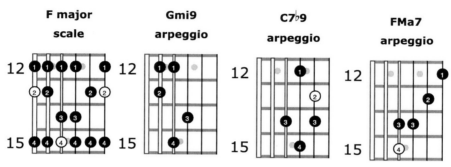

F major scale

Gmi9 arpeggio

C7♭9 arpeggio

FMa7 arpeggio

Example 31

As usual, there is chromaticism over this progression. I could have used the two-octave arpeggio from Example 24 over the F6, but in the etude and improvisation I mostly stick to the higher octave. The ii-V in E♭ in this position is like the ii-V in D♭ in Position 4 and the ii-V in F in Position 1:

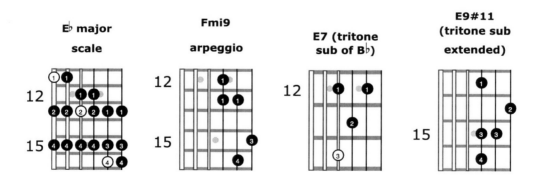

E♭ major scale

Fmi9 arpeggio

E7 (tritone sub of B♭)

E9#11 (tritone sub extended)

Example 32

I use tritone substitution on the B♭7 chord in both the etude and the improvisation. In the improvisation the E7 extends up through its M9 and #11 intervals to provide a #5 on the B♭7 in

27

addition to the ♭5 and ♭9. The material over the E♭6 in the etude is another example of a hexatonic scale: a major scale minus the perfect 4th.

The ii-V in D♭ here is like the ii-V in F in Position 2 and the ii-V in E♭ in Position 1:

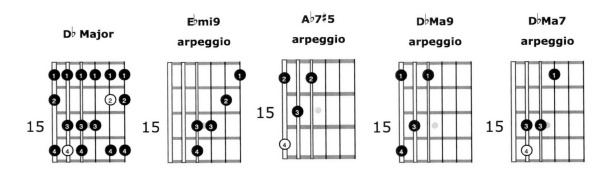

Example 33

In the etude I use an augmented sound to alter the dominant, while in the improvisation the material is more chromatic. The line in measure 11 of the etude is like the two-octave arpeggio in Example 24, but played on a lower set of strings.

For the final ii-V, I use two variations of tritone substitution, using the following shapes:

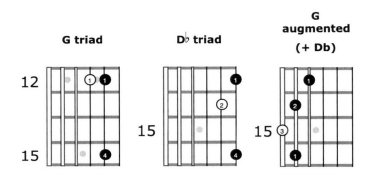

Example 34

In the etude I use alternating G and D♭ major triads, and they are phrased poly-rhythmically, as 8th notes in groups of three. In the improvisation I incorporate the note D♭ into a G augmented triad in a reference to the melody of the Dizzy Gillespie tune "A Night in Tunisia."

And that concludes this exploration of these Miles-type changes on the entire fretboard of the guitar. The next position would just be a repeat of the first, up an octave. Notice how the same shapes get used and reused in different keys and different parts of the fretboard. The efficiency of this approach has helped me to achieve fluency on the instrument. I also encourage you to analyze the etudes and improvisations for their vocabulary: chromaticism, altered dominants, over-the-barline phrasing, and other classic jazz techniques.

CHAPTER 3

Wayne-Type Changes

The chord changes in this chapter are more on the "modern" side of jazz harmony, which is a term that I interpret broadly to mean that there are modal and non-functional progressions mixed in with more standard ii-Vs and the like. Here are the chord changes:

The tune begins in F minor, although the key center that is most strongly established is C minor in bars 9-12. I would describe the progression as mostly modal, with some nods to functional harmony. The upper structure of the EMa7♯11 and G♭Ma7♯11 both contain E♭ minor triads, which helps with position playing. Bars 5-8 are perhaps the most unusual and difficult part of the progression. These chords are non-functional—they are simply individual sounds, colors. **Their use here brings to mind the famous Debussy quote: "Some people wish above all to conform to the rules, I wish only to render what I can hear. There is no theory. You have only to listen. Pleasure is the law."** I tend to use melodic minor applications and augmented ideas on these chords: B♭ Super Locrian (B melodic minor) on the B♭7♯5 to D♭ Lydian Dominant (A♭ melodic minor) on the D♭7♯11 to A♭ Lydian Augmented (F melodic minor) on the A♭Ma7♯5. **As we get into**

the specific shapes, **I will label the melodic and harmonic minor scales as such without getting into the specific modal names.** On the same three chords I could also explore the upper structures and use a B♭ augmented triad to a B augmented triad to a C major triad or dominant 7th. We will see these ideas in action soon. Bars 13-16 contain a "modal mixture." D♭ is the root throughout, but we oscillate between a Lydian Dominant sound and an Aeolian sound on the D♭mi7♯5. Here are the etude and improvisation for Position 1:

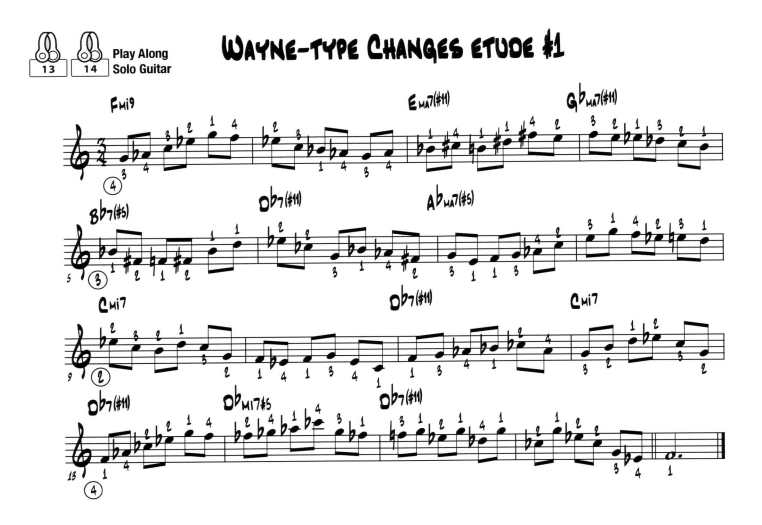

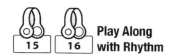
WAYNE-TYPE CHANGES IMPROV #1

I'll go through the shapes for the etude and improvisation in each position in 4-bar sections. Here are the scale and arpeggio shapes from the first four bars in Position 1, which encompasses frets 3 to 7 or so:

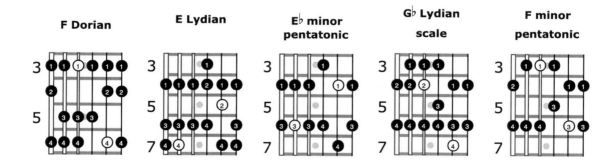

F Dorian E Lydian Eb minor pentatonic Gb Lydian scale F minor pentatonic

31

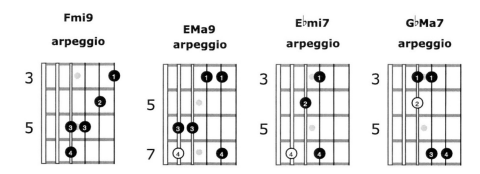

Example 35

The scale modes I use in this position are the most common, although others could work as well, such as F melodic or harmonic minor and E and G♭ Lydian Augmented. There is chromaticism in bar 4 of the etude, based on G♭ Lydian, and I tried to make the E Lydian material flow logically into the G♭ chord, with a "chromatic" approach (the notes are actually all within E Lydian). In the improvisation I imply an E♭mi7 arpeggio over the EMa7♯11—as I stated above, an EMa7♯11 arpeggio from the 7th degree gives us E♭mi7. Another option here would be to play E♭ minor pentatonic on both the EMa7♯11 and the G♭Ma7♯11, or E♭ minor pentatonic on the EMa7♯11 and F minor pentatonic on the G♭Ma7♯11. **On any Ma7♯11, a minor pentatonic down a half-step yields the very hip and relevant M7, M9, M3, ♯4, and M6 chord tones.** I have included both shapes here, and will continue to show the pentatonic shapes in each position. Here are the shapes for the next four bars:

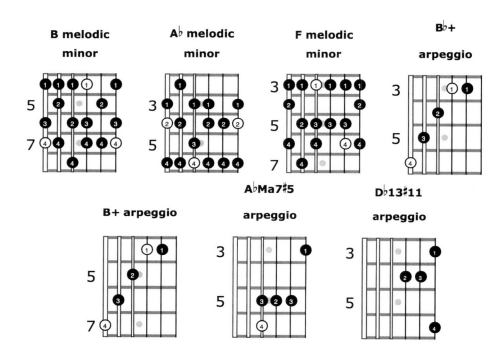

Example 36

32

In the etude I use the B♭ augmented triad to B augmented triad idea for the B♭7♯5 to D♭7♯11, as I described in the paragraph before Etude #1. B augmented is in the upper structure of D♭7♯11— if you arpeggiate from the 7th, B augmented is what you get. I don't continue directly to a C major triad or dominant 7th over the A♭Ma7♯5, although the arpeggio idea I play contains the C triad. I like the sound of an ascending series of triads against a differing bass motion—in this case B♭ to D♭ to A♭ (up a minor 3rd, down a perfect 4th). The material on the improvisation is similar, although I also use an upper structure D♭7♯11 arpeggio on beat 3 of bar 6, leading into an F melodic minor sequence in measures 7-8. The harmony of the next four bars is simpler, here are the shapes:

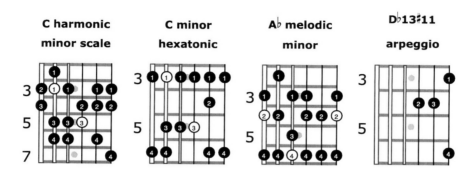

Example 37

These four bars are functional: two bars of Cmi7, one bar of D♭7♯11 (which is the tritone sub of G7 and thus functions as a dominant), then back to Cmi7 for 1 bar. I use C harmonic minor on the Cmi7 in the etude and improvisation. Some may spot a contradiction between the chord symbol and the scale choice, but with minor key areas the 6th and 7th degrees are malleable. I also included in the above shapes a six-note, hexatonic collection that I often use on Cmi chord forms. On the D♭7♯11 I use the relevant melodic minor mode and arpeggio. Here are the shapes for the final four bars:

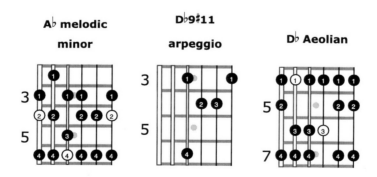

Example 38

Here is the modal mixture I spoke of in the paragraph before Etude #1. We move from D♭ Lydian Augmented, or perhaps even D♭ whole-tone, to D♭ Aeolian, a D♭mi7♯5 sound. Most of the material in the etude and improvisation is from the relevant chord-scales and arpeggios.

On to the next postiion!

Wayne-type Changes etude #2

Wayne-type Changes Improv #2

This position consists of the 5th to 10th frets. Here are the shapes for the first four bars:

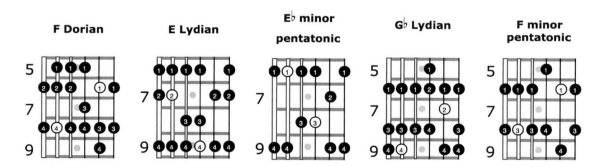

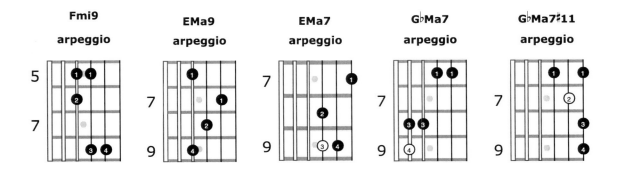

Example 39

In this position I use the same chord-scales that I used in Position 1. The arpeggio shapes here for EMa9 and GbMa7 aren't used in the etude or improvisation, but I do commonly use these shapes in this position. I also often combine the EMa9 and EMa7 arpeggios into a line like this, similar to Example 14:

Example 40

An overarching goal of mine for these four bars (in every position) is to smooth out the transition between EMa7#11 and GbMa7#11. In the etude I even anticipate an F natural on the last 16th note of bar 3—a very dissonant b9 interval on an EMa7#11, but it works!

Here are the shapes for the second four bars in this position:

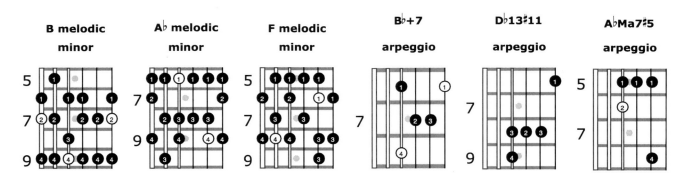

Example 41

In this position, in both the etude and the improvisation, I am relying heavily on melodic minor applications, although I am playing off a Bb augmented triad on the Bb7#5. **As in the previous chapter, you will find that as we move up the fretboard the shapes repeat.** In this instance the Db13#11 arpeggio is identical to the AbMa7#5 arpeggio from Position 1, Example 36. Here are the shapes for the next section:

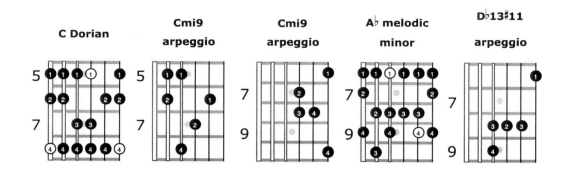

Example 42

There are some repeated shapes from Example 41, the Db13#11 for instance. Also, the arpeggio from Example 40 would work perfectly here, provided it is moved down one fret. For the last four bars I am only including the shape for the Dbmi7#5, since on the Db7#11 I again use Ab melodic minor and the Db13#11 arpeggio from Examples 41 and 42:

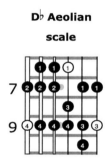

Example 43

The material in the etude and improvisation is largely scale-based with a quick arpeggiation of Db13#11 in measure 13. This leads us to the etude and improvisation in Position 3, which are on the following pages.

Wayne-type Changes Etude #3

WAYNE-TYPE CHANGES IMPROV #3

Position 3 ranges from fret 7 to fret 12; here are the shapes for the first four bars of the progression:

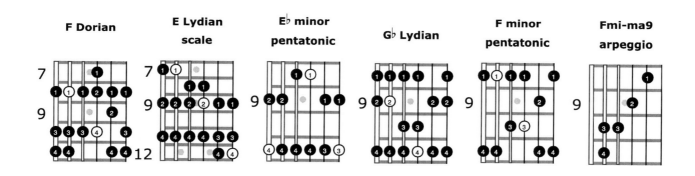

F Dorian   E Lydian   E♭ minor   F minor   Fmi-ma9
                  scale   pentatonic   G♭ Lydian   pentatonic   arpeggio

39

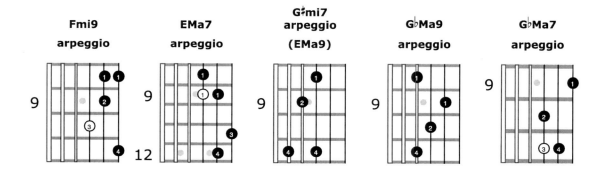

Example 44

Again, I am using the most common chord scales for this progression, although the Fmima9 arpeggio in measures 1-2 of the improvisation suggests perhaps harmonic or melodic minor. I've included some shapes that I don't use in *this* etude or improvisation, but which I commonly use in this position. I could have used the two-octave arpeggio from Example 40 here, transposed up 2 frets to the key of G♭, and I might have played a two-octave EMa7 arpeggio from the 3rd that looks like this:

Example 45

Here are shapes for the next four bars:

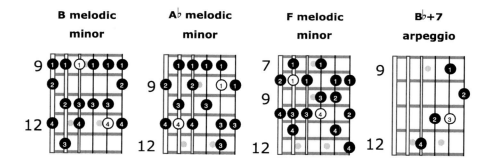

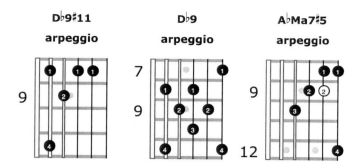

Example 46

Here again I am using melodic minor applications, and like the previous four bars I have included some shapes that don't occur specifically in the etude or improvisation—particularly the Db9 arpeggio above. This is a shape I use all the time. It is very versatile and could also be used over Fmi7b5, G7alt, Abmi6, BMa7#11, and other harmonies. Here are the C minor shapes:

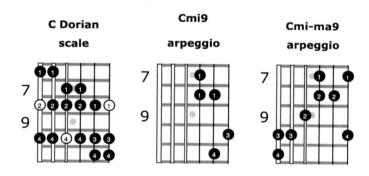

Example 47

For the Db7#11 in this 4-bar section I use the shapes from Example 46. In the etude I use this familiar Cmi9 arpeggio shape over the Cmi7, while in the improvisation I use this two-octave Cmi-ma9 arpeggio, which is nearly identical to the two-octave arpeggio in Example 20 from Chapter 2.

Once again, for the last four bars I will only give the shapes for the Dbmi7#5, since Db7#11 has been well-covered in this position:

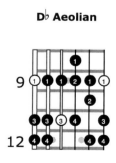

Example 48

The Db mi7#5 material in both the etude and the improvisation comes from this shape of the Db Aeolian mode. Here is Position 4:

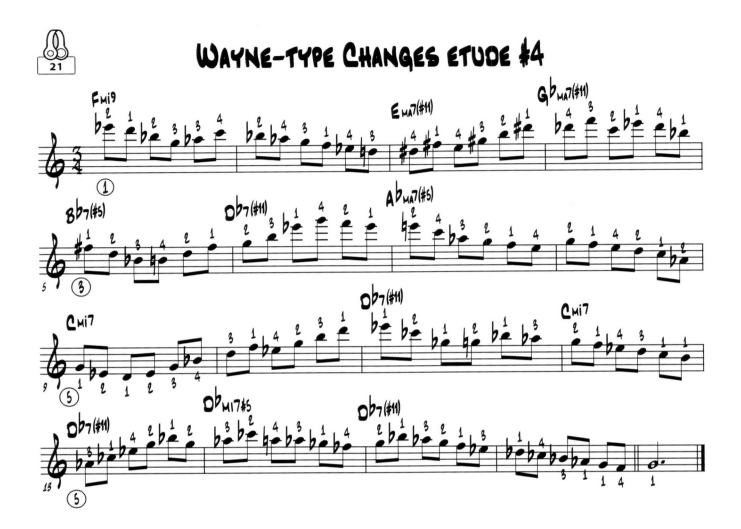

WAYNE-TYPE CHANGES ETUDE #4

WAYNE-TYPE CHANGES IMPROV #4

Position 4 contains frets 10-15. Here are the shapes for the first four bars:

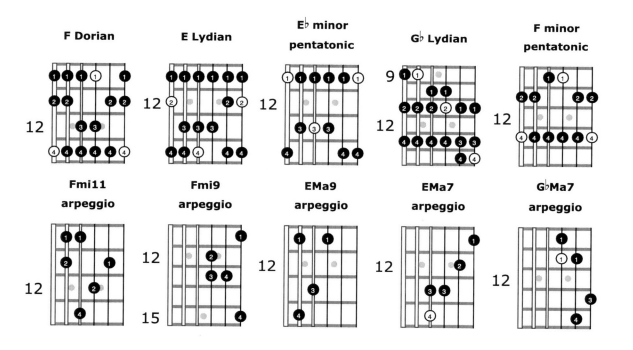

Example 49

In this position I am using F Dorian, E Lydian, and G♭ Lydian for the chord scales. Two of our familiar two-octave arpeggios could have been used here. The arpeggio from Example 14 could have been transposed up 5 frets to the Fmi9 chord, and the arpeggio from Example 24 could have been transposed up 4 frets to the EMa7♯11. Here are the next shapes:

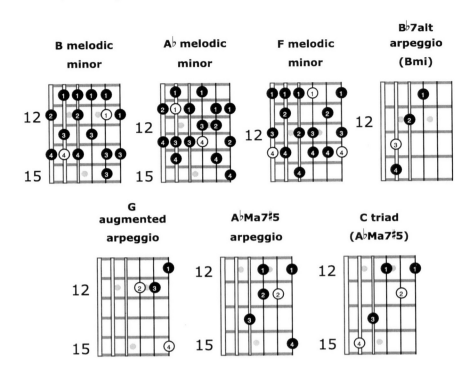

Example 50

Once again, I use the customary melodic minor applications as well as the ascending augmented triad idea. In this case, in both the etude and improvisation, the basic idea is B♭ augmented to B augmented to a C triad—with perhaps a hint of C augmented (a C triad plus A♭, the ♯5, gives you an A♭Ma7♯5 arpeggio). Here are the shapes for the next four bars:

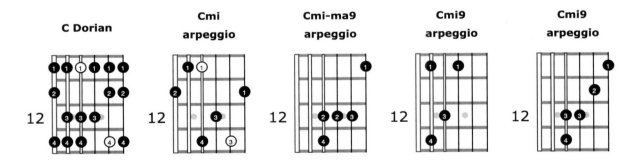

Example 51

In this position I use a variety of C minor arpeggios, including the triad arpeggio (labeled "Cmi arpeggio"), the mi-ma9 shape we've seen before, and those last two Cmi9 arpeggios which combine into the two-octave arpeggio from Example 24. The basic shapes I use over the D♭7♯11

44

are the same as in Example 50, although the line I play in measure 11 of the etude is a go-to figuration of mine. I like the shape and the contour of this idea. The same idea appears in bar 15 of the improvisation, and the final four bars of the progression use the following scale shape for the D♭mi7♯5:

D♭ Aeolian

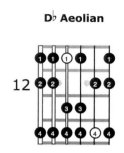

Example 52

As in previous positions, the D♭7♯11 material has been amply covered by this point. Here are the etude and improvisation for the final position:

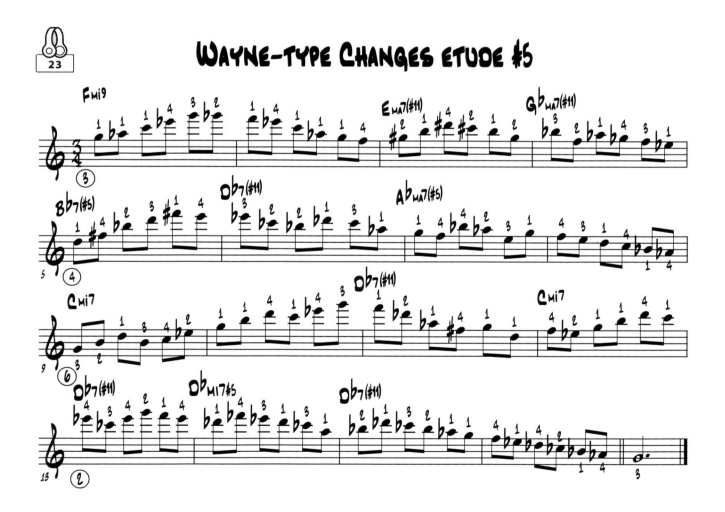

WAYNE-TYPE CHANGES ETUDE #5

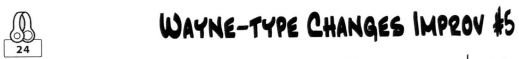

This position encompasses frets 12 to 16, after which Position 1 repeats up an octave. Here are the shapes for the first four bars:

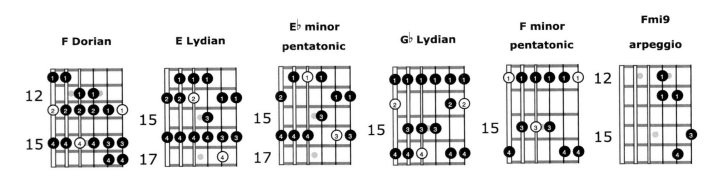

46

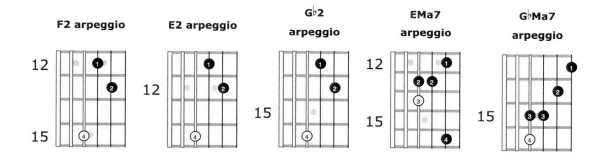

F2 arpeggio   E2 arpeggio   Gb2 arpeggio   EMa7 arpeggio   GbMa7 arpeggio

Example 53

Here are the usual chord-scale suspects, in the appropriate position. In the improvisation I use a technique that I often employ: if I encounter a particular voicing or interval structure that appeals to me I will "take it through" various scales, beginning with the major scale. With the F2, E2, and Gb2 arpeggios above, the interval structure between the 4th and 3rd strings is a 2nd, while between the 3rd and 2nd strings it is a 4th. If I observe this interval structure as I ascend and descend the length of the fretboard on particular string sets, I can make the pitches conform to various scales. For instance, if I want the F2 (made up of the notes F, G, and C) to be a sort of ii chord in Eb Major, a Dorian sound as in this chapter's progression, then the next chord as I ascend would consist of G, Ab, and D, the next notes on each string in Eb major. Here are the shapes for the Eb major scale using this interval structure on string sets 3, 2, 1 and 4, 3, 2, along with notation containing one possible rhythmic pattern to practice with the shapes. You can use this method with any interval structure, string set, or type of scale.

Strings 3, 2, 1

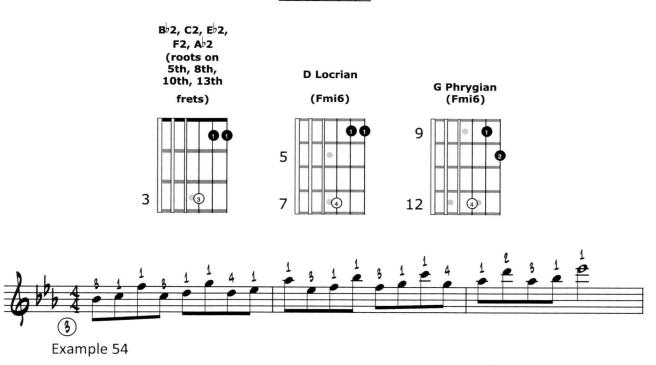

Bb2, C2, Eb2, F2, Ab2 (roots on 5th, 8th, 10th, 13th frets)   D Locrian (Fmi6)   G Phrygian (Fmi6)

Example 54

Strings 4, 3, 2

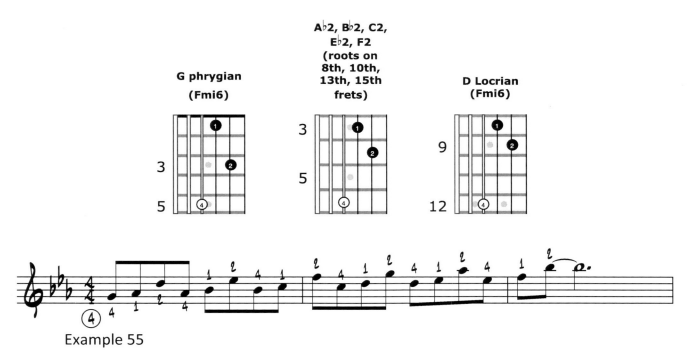

Example 55

I don't use these shapes so extensively in the improvisation or etude, but in other contexts they add a refreshing openness and modernity to my playing. Here are the shapes for the next four bars:

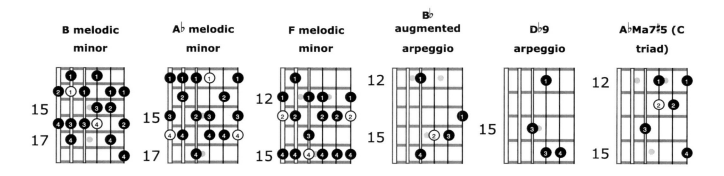

Example 56

As per usual, we have melodic minor applications, augmented triads, and a C major triad idea on the A♭Ma7♯5. On the D♭7♯11 I am mostly playing from the above D♭9 shape. The shapes for the next four bars are on the following page.

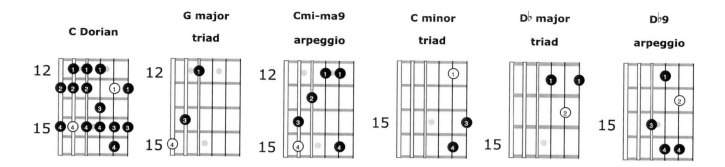

Example 57

The multi-octave Cmi-ma9 arpeggio that appears in measures 9-10 of the etude suggests C harmonic minor, but more often than not I improvise with C Dorian over this progression. A D♭ major triad appears in measure 11 of the etude, with some snaky chromaticism, while in the improvisation I play from a D♭9 arpeggio. The D♭7♯11 material in the last four bars is covered in Examples 56-57. Here is the relevant D♭ Aeolian scale shape:

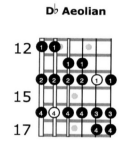

Example 58

As with the progression in Chapter 2, shapes get reused in every position, transposed to different keys. It doesn't matter that the harmony in this chapter is more "modern," and oscillates between modal and functional progressions. The method is the same, although the shapes change slightly depending on the chords of the song. Let's move on to another type of progression.

CHAPTER 4

Jobim-Type Changes

This chapter's progression is similar to the harmony in the music of the famous Brazilian composer Antonio Carlos Jobim. The changes contain a cycle of 4ths progression, some chromatically moving Ma7 chords, and a IV-I, plagal cadence. Here are just the chords:

We are in the key of Ab, and over the first four bars we descend Ab6, G6, to GbMa7, which in this case functions as an inversion of Cmi7b5, so that the progression GbMa7-F7#5-Bbmi11 is like a ii-V of ii in the key of Ab. The Dbmi6 chord in measure 7 functions as a subdominant minor progression, a minor iv-I. I learned about minor iv-I progressions from Hank Mackie many years ago, but in this case, the I chord is instead a dominant III, C7. III or iii chords can be substituted for I chords, and often are. From the C7 we have a cycle of 4ths progression that goes all the way to Db7 before resolving IV-I back to AbMa7. Many jazz progressions contain these cycles of 4ths. Some other famous examples are "Yesterdays," "Up a Lazy River," and "Sweet Georgia Brown." The etude and improvisation for Position 1 are on the following pages.

JOBIM-TYPE CHANGES ETUDE #1

51

Jobim-type Changes Improv #1

This first position consists of frets 2 to 7. As in Chapter 3, I will go through the scale and arpeggio shapes in 4-bar sections. Here are the shapes for measures 1-4 of the etude and improvisation:

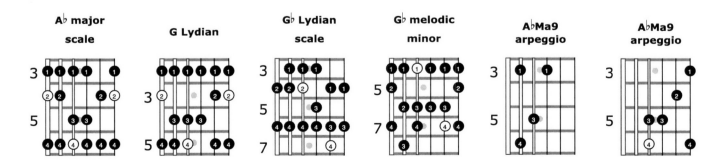

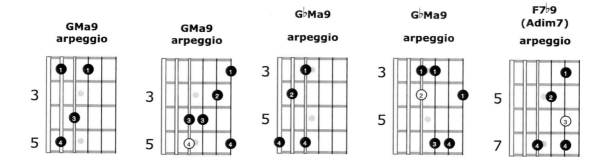

Example 59

For the I chord, A♭6, I'm thinking A♭ major, while for the following two major chords I play from a Lydian sound. Much of the time I'm not really thinking of 7-note scales, rather pentatonic collections and arpeggios with chromaticism. For the F7#5 I generally use a melodic minor scale up a half-step, in this case G♭ melodic minor, or a B♭ harmonic minor scale, which you can find below in Example 62. The arpeggios for the A♭ and G major chords could be combined into two-octave arpeggios, as in Example 24, while the G♭Ma9 arpeggios could be combined like this:

Example 60

Here are some pentatonic shapes that could work for those first three chords:

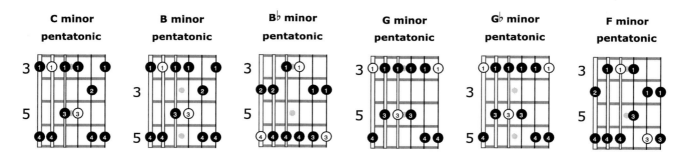

Example 61

The first three shapes above provide the M3, P5, M6, M7, M9 intervals while the last three shapes express a more Lydian sound: M7, M9, M3, #11, M6. As you can see, there are several options for just the first four bars of this progression! The shapes for the next phrase are on the following page.

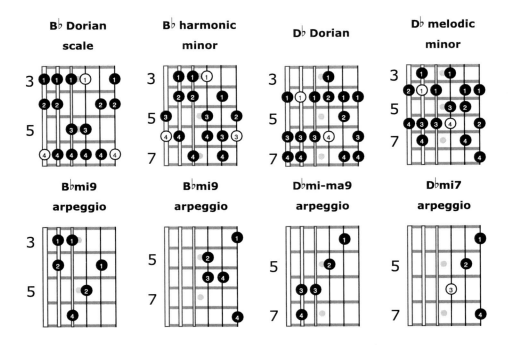

Example 62

I tend to treat the B♭mi11 as either a Dorian or harmonic minor sound, and the minor iv chord, the D♭mi6, as either Dorian or melodic minor. There are of course other options. The B♭mi9 arpeggios could be combined into a two-octave arpeggio as in Example 14 (Chapter 2), while in measure 7 of the etude the D♭mi-ma9 and D♭mi7 shapes actually do combine as just such a two-octave shape. Here are the first four bars of the dominant cycle:

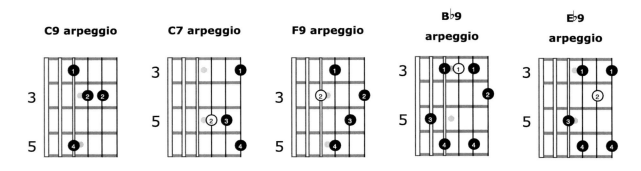

Example 63

I could write a book on dominant cycle progressions alone, so forgive me if I don't go through every possible shape in this position. **Scale-wise I could use any of the Mixolydian, half-whole diminished, Super Locrian, or other dominant scales that fit any of these four chords.** The above shapes provide the more consonant, non-altered tones for each dominant. The tritone sub and augmented triad shapes for each chord in this position follow.

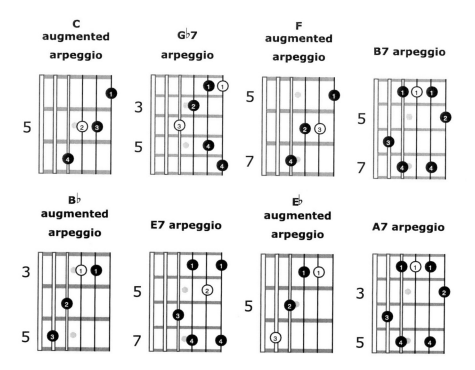

Example 64

I don't use all of these shapes in the etude and improvisation—in fact, my lines are mostly chromatic ornamentation of the more consonant shapes from Example 63—but I *could* use any of them. I will continue to provide these augmented and tritone substitutes for each subsequent position. Here are the shapes for the last four bars:

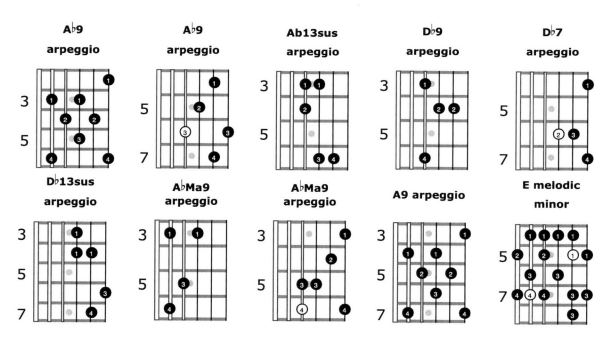

Example 65

Again the possibilities for the dominants are numerous, and I could have played a D7 arpeggio or A♭ augmented triad on the A♭7—or any of the altered scales that fit that chord. The above two-octave A♭9 and A9 arpeggios (which also appear in Example 46 in Chapter 2) are fun to play because you can use legato technique (hammer-ons and pull-offs) on the strings that contain two notes. For the A♭Ma7 in bar 15 of both the etude and improvisation, I am using the same material I used in measure 1. The last chord, the A7♯11, is a tritone substitute of E♭7, the V chord in A♭, and I usually use melodic minor harmony over it, such as the Lydian Dominant scale (the 4th mode of E melodic minor). On to the next position!

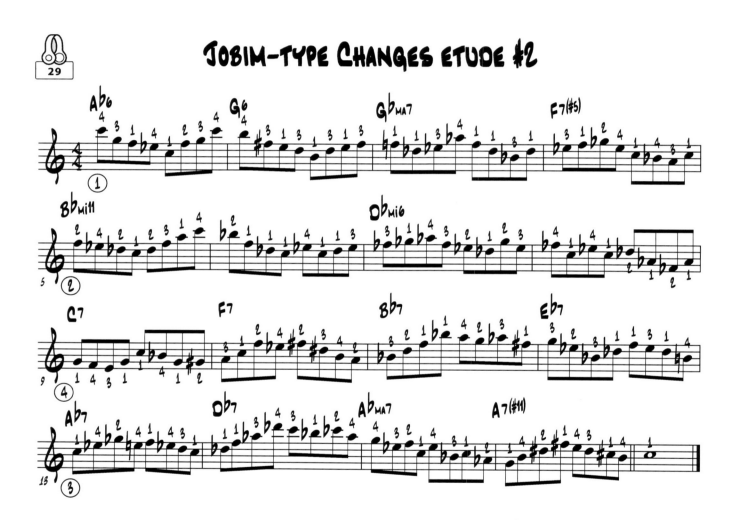

56

JOBIM-TYPE CHANGES IMPROV #2

This position covers the 4th to 10th frets, and again there are numerous shapes to go along with the harmony. The major and pentatonic scale shapes for the first three major chords are on the following page.

57

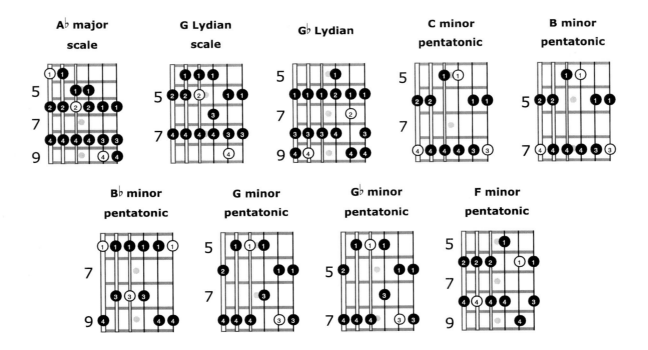

Example 66

I've ordered these pentatonic shapes as I did in Example 61: three pentatonics that yield M3, P5, M6, M7, and M9 on each chord followed by three that offer a Lydian sound: M7, M9, M3, ♯11, and M6. Here are the arpeggio shapes for the major chords and the scale and arpeggio options for the F7♯5:

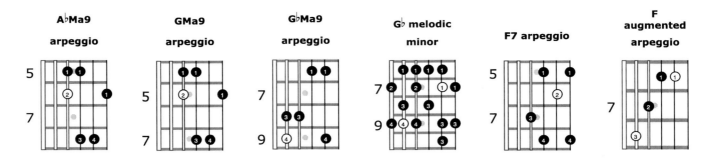

Example 67

In the etude I play off these shapes using a quartal approach, characterized by 4th intervals. The F7♯5 in the etude is perhaps more of a B♭ harmonic minor sound than the G♭ melodic minor above, although F Super Locrian is also a common choice for F7♯5. We will see the B♭ harmonic minor shape in the following example.

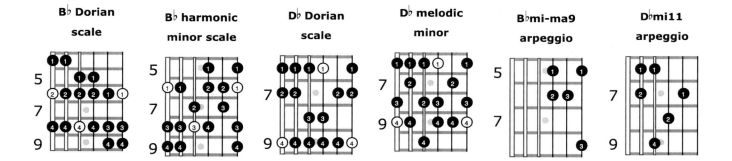

Example 68

Here is the B♭ harmonic minor scale in this position, which could be used on the F7♯5 in measure 4. I often use the Dorian mode over these minor chords as well. Furthermore, I could have used the two-octave mi-ma7 arpeggio from Example 20, back in Chapter 2—transposed to B♭ minor of course. Measure 8 of the improvisation contains a little melody that I hear at times in the playing of Wes Montgomery, Steve Masakowski, and others. Here come the dominant cycles:

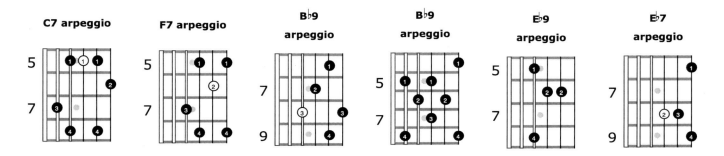

Example 69

Again, I am simplifying here. I haven't included the four Mixolydian scales, not to mention Super Locrian or half-whole diminished. These are the consonant dominant 7th arpeggios that I am ornamenting with chromaticism in the etude and improvisation. Mirroring Examples 63 and 64 above, here are the tritone subs and augmented triads for each of these dominants:

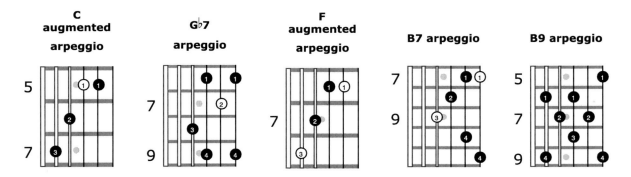

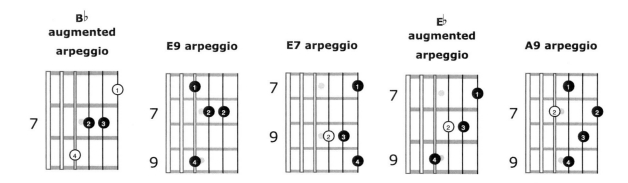

Example 70

I don't always alter all the dominants, but it is good to know where the grips are for augmented triads and tritone subs. **Already after two positions we can see that the shapes are repeating. With sequences of dominants in different areas of the fretboard this repetition is noticed quickly.** Here are the shapes for the last four bars:

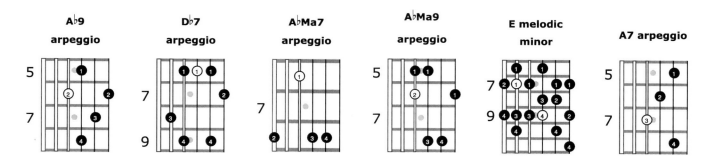

Example 71

Over the Ab7 and Db7 one could also use Ab and Db Mixolydian, or any of the alterations from the previous four bars. The AbMa7 arpeggio in bar 15 of the improvisation is an inversion that I like to use to break up the contour of my playing. Skipping the 5th string and using wide intervals makes a nice change. On the following pages we continue with the Position 3 etude and improvisation.

Jobim-Type Changes Etude #3

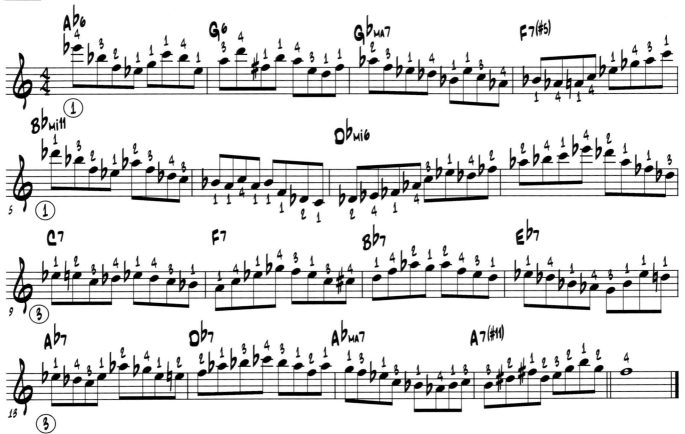

Jobim-type Changes Improv #3

This position includes frets 7 to 11 or so. The scale shapes for the first four bars are on the following page.

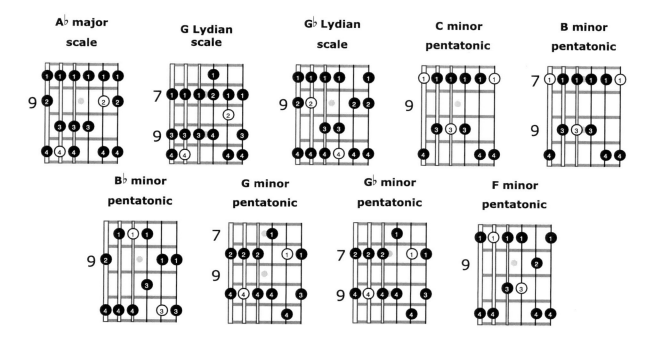

Example 72

I'm using quartal sounds again in both the etude and the improvisation, especially over the first two chords. Here are the rest of the scale and arpeggio shapes for the first four bars:

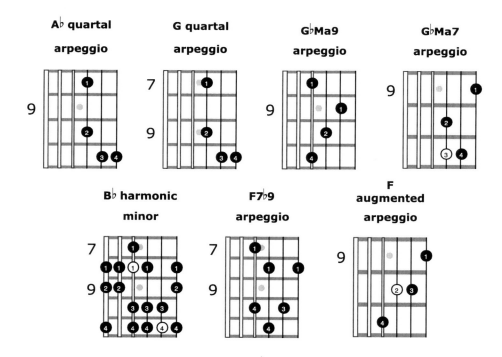

Example 73

Example 73 above contains the basic shapes for the quartal material in bars 1-2 of the etude and improvisation. This quartal approach comes naturally on the guitar since the strings are tuned in 4th intervals. On the F7♯5 everything is coming from B♭ harmonic minor rather than

Gb melodic minor. In the etude I play from an F7b9 arpeggio, while in the improvisation I use an F augmented triad. Here are the next four bars:

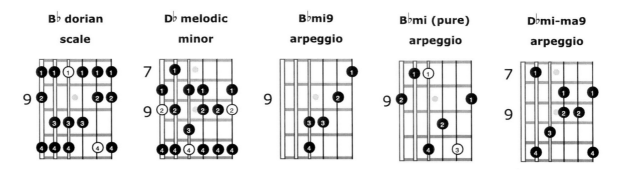

Example 74

The Bbmi11 material oscillates between Dorian and harmonic minor, while the Dbmi6 uses both Dorian and melodic minor. The Dbmi-ma9 arpeggio from measures 7-8 of the etude is nearly identical to Example 20 from Chapter 2. Here are the dominant cycle shapes:

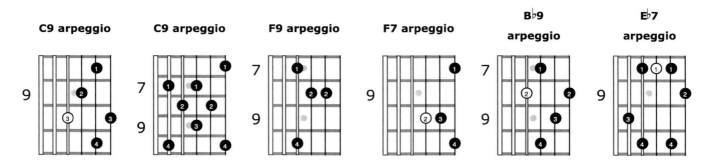

Example 75

The shapes are repeating in every position, in a slightly different order. Here are the tritone subs and augmented triads for this position:

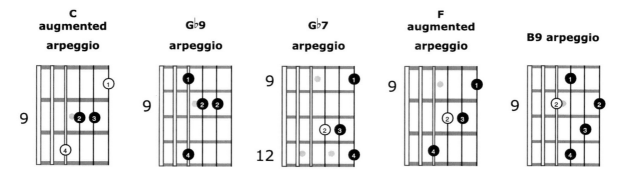

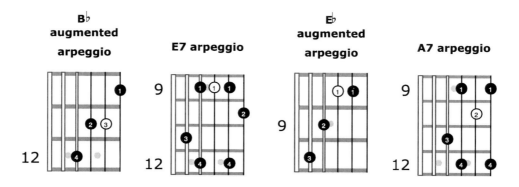

Example 76

In the etude and improvisation I am using chromatic ornamentation of the Example 75 shapes, along with some five eighth-note resolution cells (in measure 9 of the etude in particular), but these Example 76 shapes are very useful for altering the dominants in this position. Here are the last four bars:

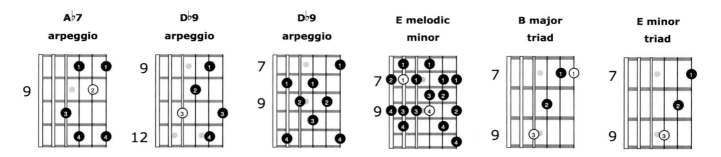

Example 77

The last two dominants of the cycle are treated with chromaticism around these shapes, while the A7♯11 gets the E melodic minor, Lydian Dominant treatment. In measure 16 of both the etude and the improvisation I combine a B major triad and an E minor triad, which brings out the Lydian Dominant sound with a triadic rather than scalar contour. The A♭Ma7 is treated the same as in the first measure of the progression. The etude and improvisation for Position 4 follow on the next two pages.

65

Jobim-type Changes etude #4

66

Jobim-type Changes Improv #4

This position covers frets 9 to 15, more or less. Read on for the scale shapes for the first four bars.

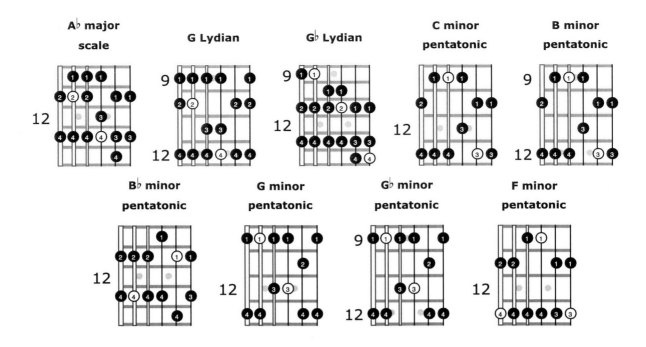

Example 78

The material in this position is more tertian, and the above scale shapes cover most of what happens in the etude and improvisation, but here are the arpeggios for the major chords and the scales and arpeggios for the F7♯5:

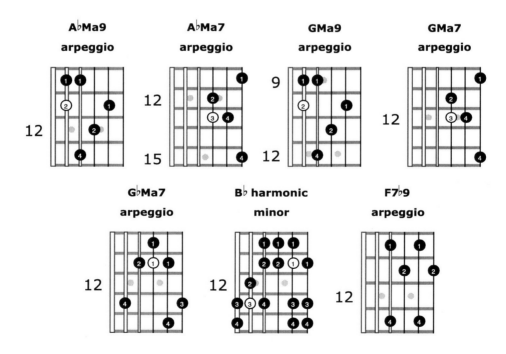

Example 79

The A♭Ma9 and GMa9 arpeggios could be combined similarly to Example 14 back in Chapter 2, and the G♭Ma7 arpeggio could be played like Example 45 from Chapter 3. The F7♯5 gets the B♭ harmonic minor treatment along with an F7♭9 arpeggio, very much like the previous position. Here are the shapes for the next four bars:

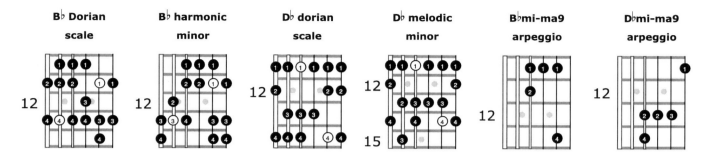

Example 80

In this position, the B♭mi11 is treated with both Dorian and harmonic minor, while the D♭mi6 receives Dorian and melodic minor. Here are the dominant cycles:

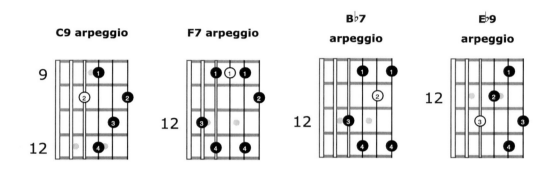

Example 81

These shapes should be very familiar by now. Here are the augmented and tritone substitutions:

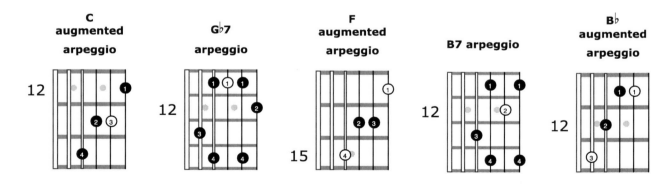

69

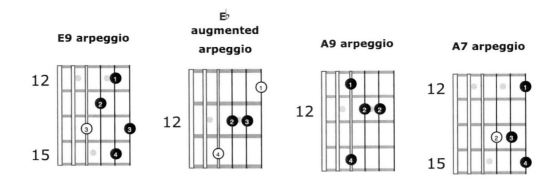

Example 82

Again, same concept, same shapes—different order. Here are the shapes for the last four bars:

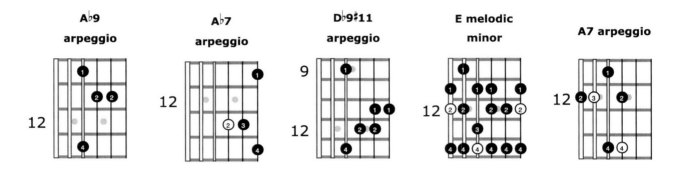

Example 83

The shapes for A♭7 are familiar, while the D♭9♯11 arpeggio is a variation on something we've also seen before. In the etude the A7♯11 uses an A7 arpeggio voiced on the lowest strings—the low strings have a different timbre, and it's nice to get down there every now and again. Position 5 follows.

JOBIM-TYPE CHANGES ETUDE #5

71

JOBIM-TYPE CHANGES IMPROV #5

This position encompasses frets 12 to 17 or so. Here are the scales for the first three chords:

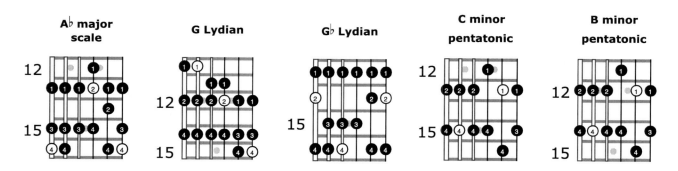

Ab major scale   G Lydian   Gb Lydian   C minor pentatonic   B minor pentatonic

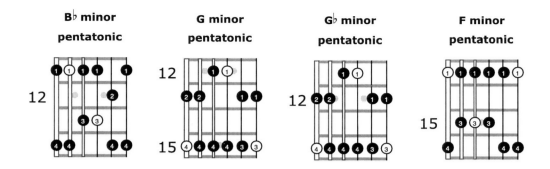

Example 84

Here are the arpeggios for the major chords and the scales and arpeggio shapes for the F7♯5:

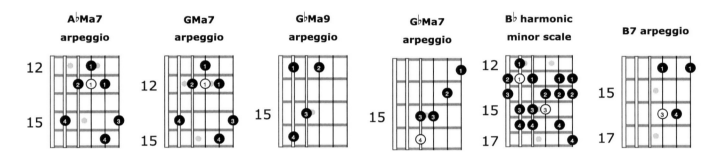

Example 85

The arpeggios for A♭Ma7 and GMa7 are very similar to Example 45 in Chapter 3, in both the etude and the improvisation (minus the chromatic approach to the 3rd), while the G♭Ma7 is treated similarly to Example 24 from Chapter 2. Measure 4 of the improvisation plays off a tritone sub, and emphasizes the ♭5/♯11 interval. Here are the shapes for the next four bars:

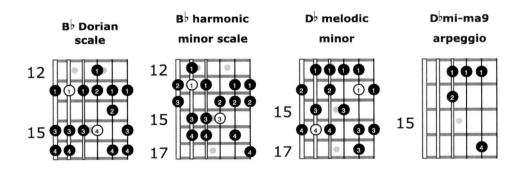

Example 86

The etude and the improvisation are very scalar, except for the D♭mi-ma9 arpeggio in measure 8 of the etude. There are other shapes and arpeggios that I could have used, but I think by this point we have enough shapes to work with on this progression! Here are the dominant cycles:

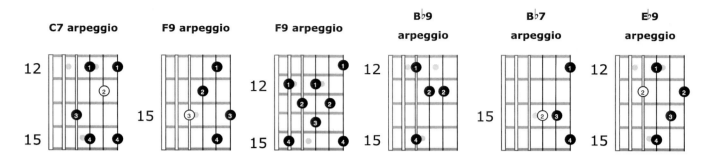

Example 87

These shapes have all been used before. Hopefully by this point in the book you can recognize them. Here are the augmented shapes and tritone substitutes:

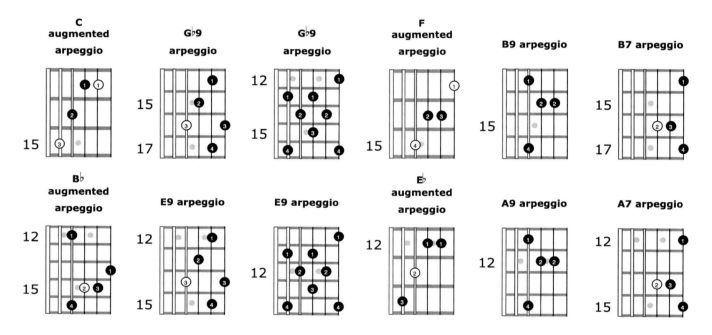

Example 88

More repetition, although the B♭ augmented arpeggio is a variation we haven't used as frequently. Read on for the last four bars.

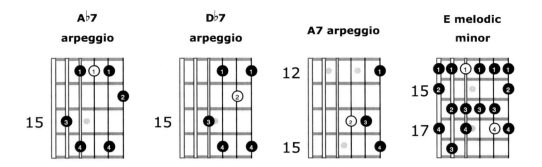

Example 89

Common shapes again, although the A7♯11 material straddles Position 4 and perhaps Position 1 in the higher octave. **In the heat of battle, when improvising, I don't really stick to specific positions anymore, so in some of these improvisation examples my fingerings don't conform exactly to the shapes; my departure from strict position playing occurs because I'm used to moving fluidly up and the down the length of the fretboard.**

We have now covered a progression full of dominant cycles, with constant repetition of shapes, which should be expected by this point.

CHAPTER 5

Monk-Type Changes

The progression in this chapter has unusual phrasing and some non-functional harmonic resolutions, but fewer chords than in any progression we have encountered thus far. Here are the etude and improvisation on these Thelonious Monk-type changes in Position 1:

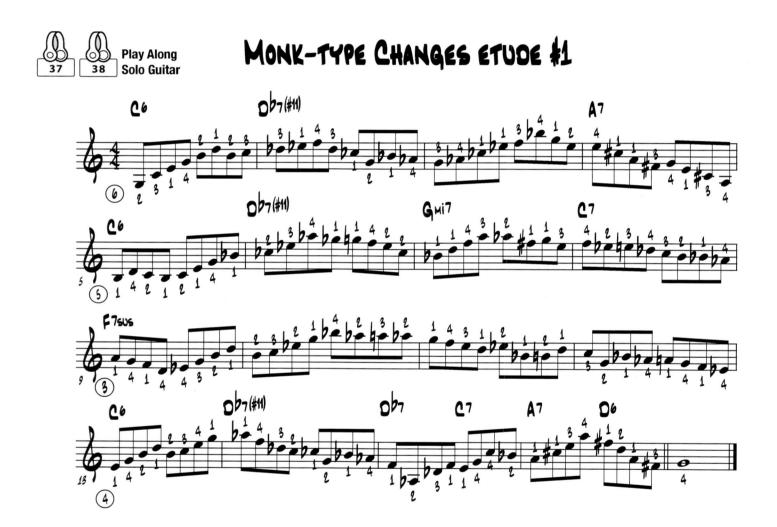

MONK-TYPE CHANGES IMPROV #1

The A7 in measure 4 does not go back to C6 in measure 5 through any sort of tonic-dominant relationship that I'm familiar with. Likewise, the progression resolves to D6 at the end of each chorus, then promptly returns to C6 with no preparation. The rest of the tune is fairly straight-forward, and there is a nice 4-bar stretch where you can explore F7sus stress-free. As with the last two progressions, I'll break this tune down into 4-bar sections. This first position is made up of frets 2 to 6. Here are the shapes I use over the first four bars of the etude and improvisation:

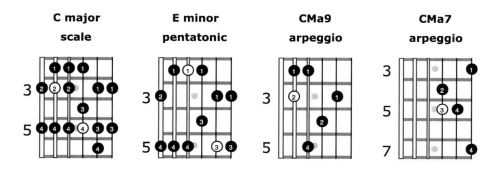

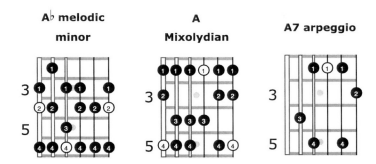

Ab melodic minor   A Mixolydian   A7 arpeggio

Example 90

By this point, all these shapes have been seen before. Over the C6 I use the major scale and the "minor pentatonic from the third" that we explored in detail in the last chapter. I also use the CMa9 and CMa7 arpeggio shapes that can combine into the idea we first encountered in Example 45 back in Chapter 3. Db7♯11 gets the melodic minor treatment, the so-called Lydian Dominant scale, the 4th mode of Ab melodic minor. Then the A7 is outlined with simple arpeggios and chromatic bebop gestures. I find in this progression that the A7 comes as such a surprise that it is most effective to play over it very simply and clearly. Here are the next four bars' shapes:

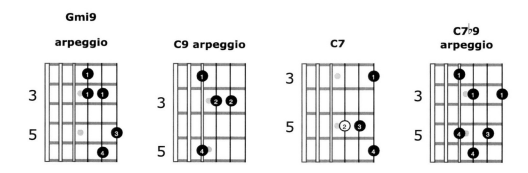

Gmi9 arpeggio   C9 arpeggio   C7   C7b9 arpeggio

Example 91

I treat the C6 and Db7♯11 in this 4-bar phrase identically to the previous four bars, so there is no need to reprint the same shapes. Bars 7-8 contain a ii-V in F, and the shapes are basically the same as those in Example 8 from Chapter 2. The next four bars are all F7sus. Here are the shapes I use in this position:

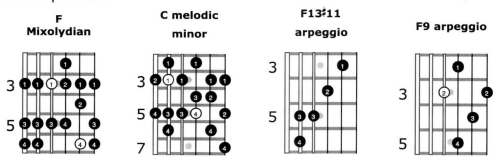

F Mixolydian   C melodic minor   F13♯11 arpeggio   F9 arpeggio

Example 92

In addition to the above shapes, I use a great deal of chromaticism around the chord tones of F7sus—and F7 more broadly. As I have previously stated, **these etudes and improvisations should also be studied for their musical and artistic value, beyond the subjects of positions and shapes.** Here are the shapes for the last four bars:

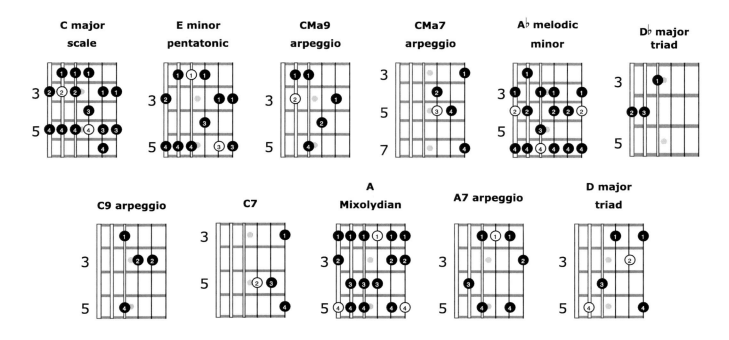

Example 93

Most of the chords in these four bars have already occurred, and the shapes are the same, but I thought I'd repeat some as a courtesy. The Db7 in measure 15 of the etude is outlined by a simple, low-register major triad. The last two bars of this progression contain a more rapid harmonic rhythm, two chords per bar, and I often use simple triads, perhaps with some chromatic ornamentation, so that I can play these changes *efficiently*. The etude and improvisation for Position 2 follow on the next two pages.

MONK-TYPE CHANGES ETUDE #2

MONK-TYPE CHANGES IMPROV #2

This position encompasses frets 4 to 8. Here are the shapes for the first four bars:

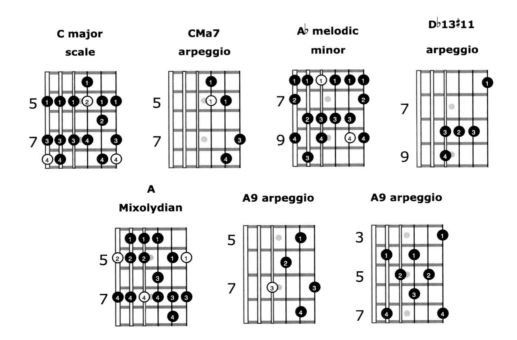

Example 94

As with the first position, the Db7#11 receives the melodic minor, Lydian Dominant treatment, and there is a healthy serving of chromaticism throughout. The A7 is arpeggiated with some ornamentation reminiscent of the dominant cycles in the Jobim-type changes from Chapter 4. Here are the shapes for the next four bars:

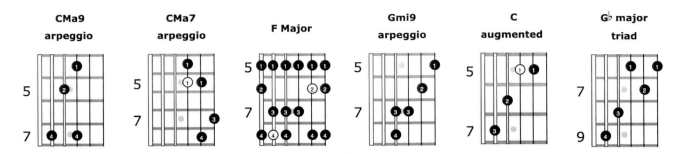

Example 95

The Db7#11 material is the same as in measures 2-3. The C6 material in measure 5 of the etude is similar to the two-octave arpeggio in Example 45 from Chapter 3. The C7 is treated with an augmented triad in the etude and a Gb major triad, a tritone substitution, in the improvisation. Here are the F7sus shapes:

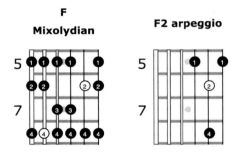

Example 96

Most of what I play in the etude and improvisation on this harmony comes from the Mixolydian scale, with classic jazz chromaticism around the chord tones of the F7sus. I use this F2 arpeggio in measure 12 of the improvisation. In measure 9 of the etude and the improvisation I allude to a 4-note cell that I often play more literally over this harmony. Here is the cell, in this position:

Example 97

Over this harmony, the four pitches D, E♭, G, and A form a sort of F13 cell, but due to the commonality of chord tones you could also use these exact notes over a Cmi6, an E♭Ma7♯11 or Ma7♯5, an Ami7♭5, a D7sus♭9, or a B7alt—a very versatile collection! Here are the shapes for the last four bars:

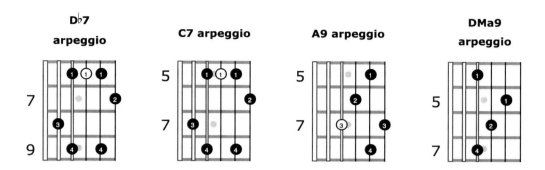

Example 98

The C6 and D♭7♯11 material has already been covered. During the two-chord per bar finish of the form I use the above shapes, but **the chromaticism in these last four bars should be studied and emulated if one wants to become fluent in classic jazz vocabulary.** Here are the etude and improvisation for Position 3:

MONK-TYPE CHANGES ETUDE #3

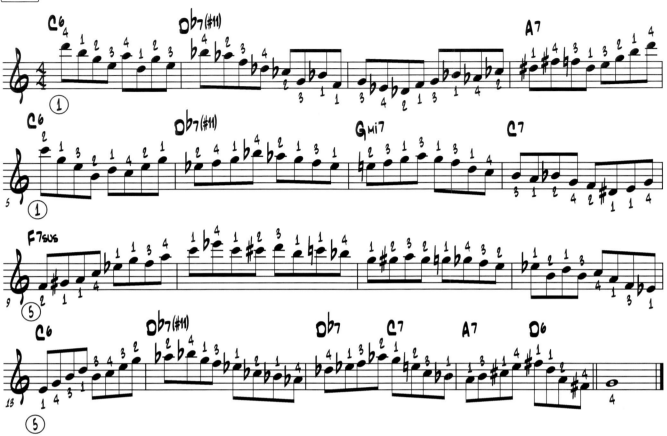

MONK-TYPE CHANGES IMPROV #3

This position is made up of frets 7 to 11 or so. Here are the shapes for the first four bars:

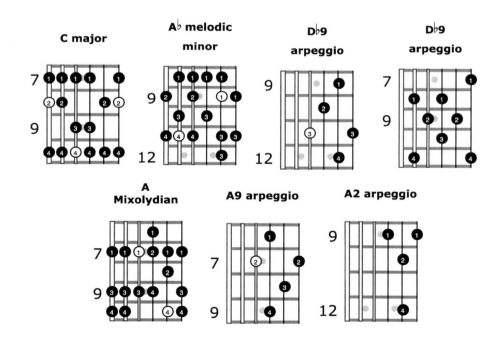

Example 99

The chords here are treated similarly to the previous 2 positions, and we are starting to see some repetition of the shapes, which is of course the point of this book. The C6 and D♭7♯11 in the next four bars use the shapes from Example 99, but here are the compatible Gmi7 and C7 scale shapes:

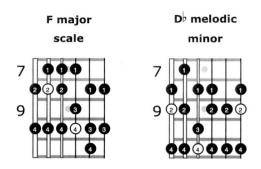

Example 100

The material in the etude and improvisation in this position is very scalar. If you want to explore some more arpeggio-based material for this position, see Example 21 from Chapter 2, which addresses the same harmony. Measure 8 of the improvisation contains a classic nine eighth-note resolution cell, although the first beat consists of a quarter note instead of two eighths. Here is the F7sus material:

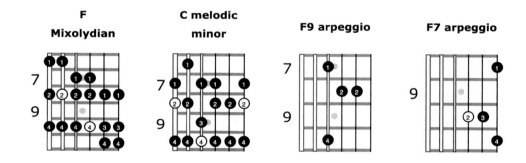

Example 101

The improvisation and especially the etude are highly chromatic, with ornamentation of the F7sus chord tones. By now this should be expected! The shapes used in the final four measures are shown on the next page.

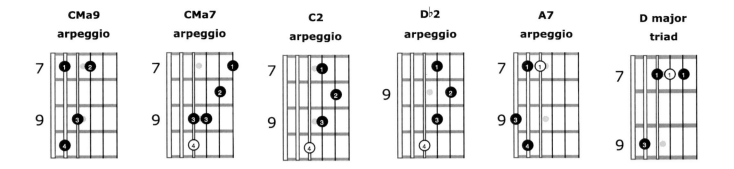

Example 102

As with previous positions, many of the shapes used in these four bars have already been covered. I use a variation of Example 24, the two-octave CMa9 arpeggio from Chapter 2, in measure 13 of the etude. The C2 and D♭2 "arpeggios" above haven't really come up yet, although this 4-note cell is very common in jazz improvisation, especially in the 1960s Coltrane/McCoy Tyner era. Here are the etude and improvisation for the next position:

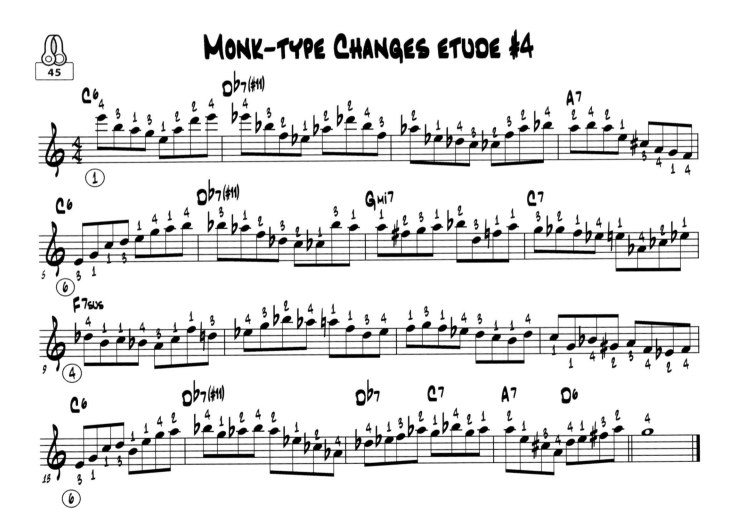

MONK-TYPE CHANGES IMPROV #4

This position covers frets 9 to 13, more or less. Here are the shapes for the first four bars of the etude and improvisation:

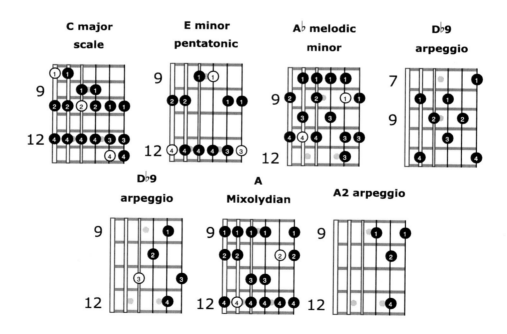

Example 103

The C6 material is quartal in nature, coming from the C major scale, or really E minor pentatonic. I'm using the same shapes over the Db7#11 that I used in the last position. This is one of those in-between spots on the fretboard, and it seemed logical to reuse the Position 3 shapes, at least for the Db7#11. I took a different approach on the improvisation, going for Monk-esque rhythmic ideas rather than my usual long lines. Here are the shapes for the next four bars:

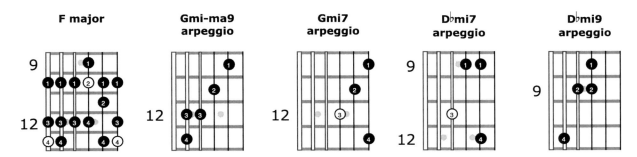

Example 104

In both the etude and improvisation, the C6 and Db7#11 use the shapes from Example 103, while the ii-V in F uses chromatic ornamentation of arpeggios along with a tritone substitute of the ii chord, a technique that goes back to Example 22 in Chapter 2 and the improvisation over Miles-type changes in Position 3. Also, in both the etude and the improvisation the resolution to F7sus goes over-the-barline, again echoing the Miles-type changes in the 3rd position. Here are the F7sus shapes:

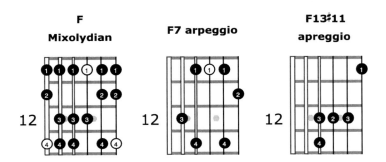

Example 105

In this position I use scale-based chromaticism and some arpeggio shapes that we have seen time and again over previous progressions. The shapes for the final four bars are on the following page.

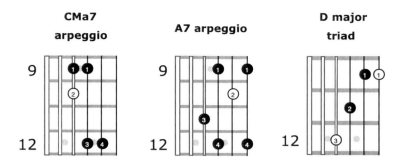

CMa7 arpeggio   A7 arpeggio   D major triad

Example 106

Most of the shapes that I use here have been covered, including the D♭2 and D2 arpeggios that I play in measures 15-16 of the etude—you can find them in Example 102 above. In measure 15 of the improvisation I anticipate the C7 by one beat. This is unusual, since I usually extend harmony over-the-barline in the opposite direction, but we will see more of these anticipations in the next chapter. But now for the final position of this progression:

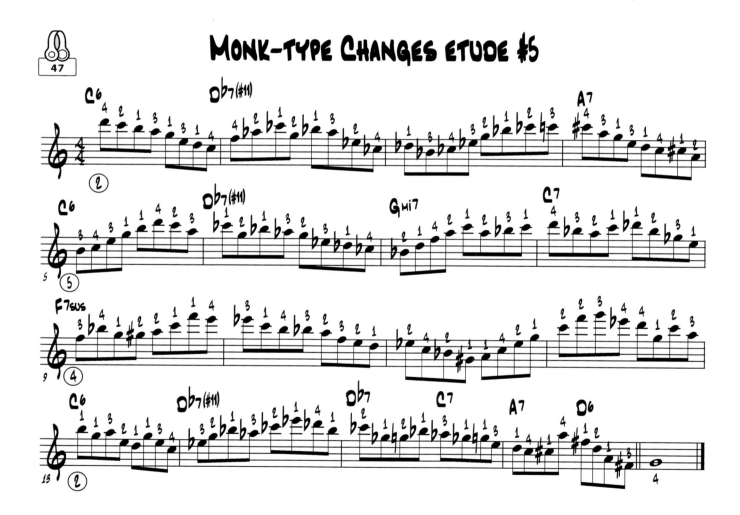

MONK-TYPE CHANGES ETUDE #5

90

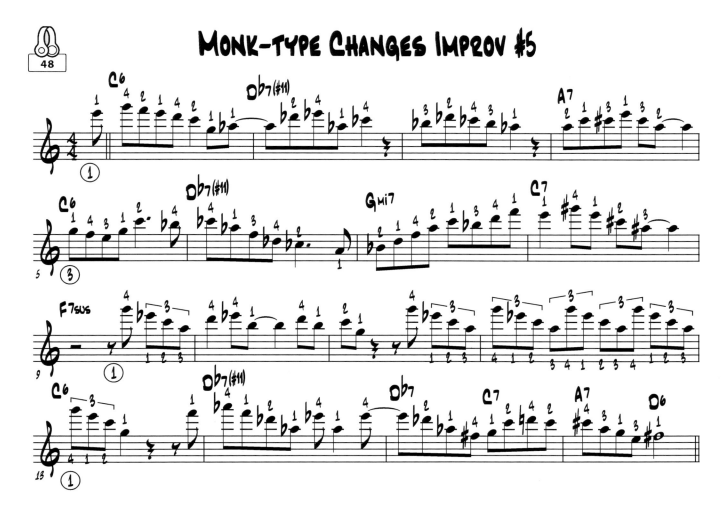

This final position encompasses frets 11 to 15. Here are the shapes for the first four bars of the etude and improvisation:

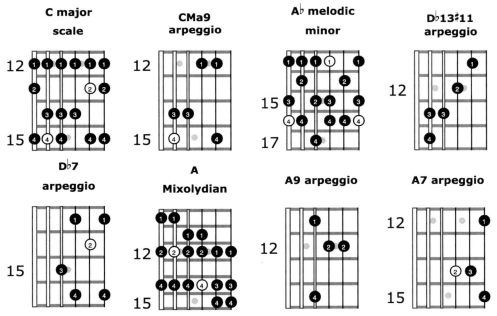

Example 107

The C6 material is very scalar here, while the Db7#11 straddles two positions—the two arpeggio shapes combined with Ab melodic minor cover six frets! Here are the next four bars' shapes:

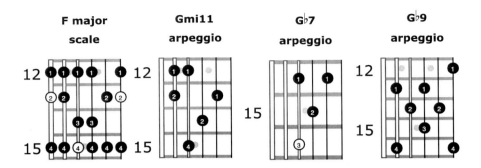

Example 108

The C6 material is similar to measure 1, and the Db7#11 again straddles two positions in the etude and improvisation. The C7 is altered with a pair of tritone substitutions, using the shapes above that we've seen many times before. Here is the F7sus material:

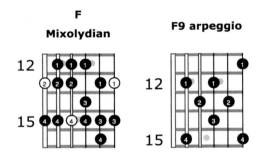

Example 109

The etude contains some snaky, classic jazz chromaticism, outlining the F7 chord and using the Mixolydian scale. In the improvisation I am using the above F9 arpeggio to execute a rhythmic idea I learned from Herbie Hancock, specifically from a passage of his solo on "My Funny Valentine" from the 1964 Miles Davis concert, captured on the albums *My Funny Valentine* and *'Four & More.'* It's basically triplets in groupings of 4. Herbie plays it around 12:40-12:47 on the recording I have.

In the last four bars there is nothing new, shape-wise, but there is much idiomatic chromaticism, and in measure 15 of the etude I extend the Db7 one beat into the C7, the converse of the last position's improvisation.

In this chapter, another progression has been explored on the entire fretboard of the guitar, with a set of shapes that recur again and again, transposed to different keys. We have one more progression to go, a highly complex harmonic puzzle with chords that change every two beats.

CHAPTER 6

Trane-Type Changes

The progression that we explore in Chapter 6 is a variation of the cycle of key centers moving in major thirds that John Coltrane used often in the late 1950s and early 1960s. These changes are particularly difficult due to the harmonic rhythm of one chord every two beats. Let's dive right in. Here are the etude and improvisation in Position 1, covering frets 2 to 7:

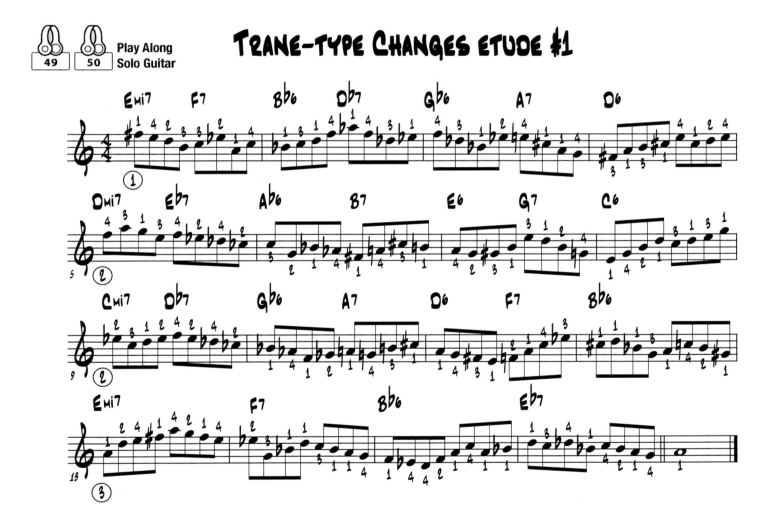

93

TRANE-TYPE CHANGES IMPROV #1

I will go through the shapes for this progression in 4-bar sections. Even though the harmonic rhythm is more rapid, there are certain similarities with the Jobim-type changes from Chapter 4. The harmonic cycles don't follow the cycle of 4ths, but there are dominant chords in nearly every bar, yielding a plethora of dominant 7th arpeggios; I use the same ones here as in Chapter 4. For the measures that contain two chords, I am not really thinking *scale shapes*; rather, I am *ornamenting the arpeggios*—or in some cases just using *fragments of the arpeggios*. Here are the shapes for the first four bars of the above etude and improvisation:

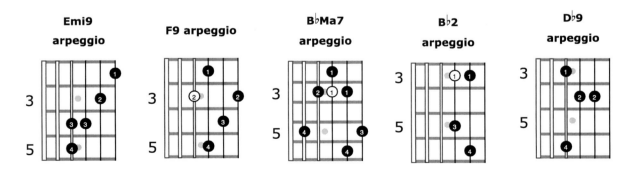

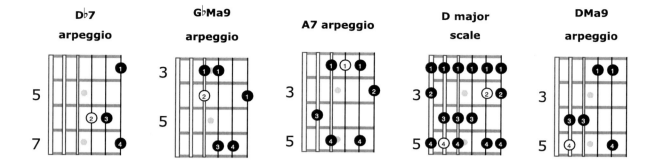

Example 110

I anticipate the F7 in measure 1 of the improvisation. Anticipating the dominants in these Coltrane cycles is effective, but I'm not sure why. I picked up the idea from Barry Harris, who has a great video on "Giant Steps" where he argues that one should play one beat of the major chord and three beats of the subsequent dominant in each measure with a two-chord per bar harmonic rhythm. The idea works on tunes like "Giant Steps," "Satellite," "Countdown," "26-2," and even "Central Park West," but the concept doesn't translate to any other progressions that I am aware of. Other than that, I'm simply arpeggiating the chords and trying to connect things as smoothly as possible. Here are the shapes for the next four bars:

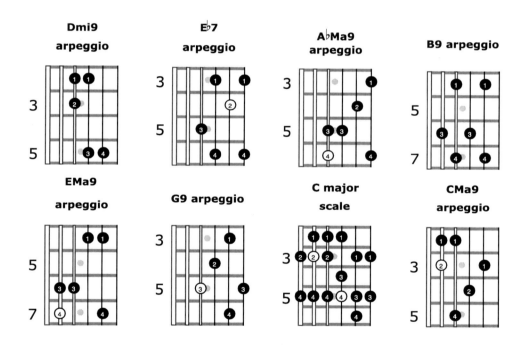

Example 111

Again, to "make" all these changes I'm using small fragments of arpeggios and ornamenting them with chromatism and some notes from the relevant chord-scale. It is a simple method, applied over an extremely complex harmonic framework. Read on for the next four bars' shapes.

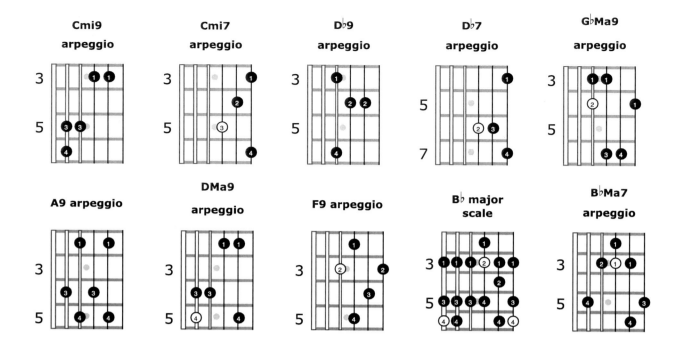

Example 112

Already, some of the chords are repeating. For this progression I'll go ahead and list the shapes again, since there is so much movement, even in a single position. In the last four bars the harmonic rhythm slows to one chord per bar. Here are the scale and arpeggio shapes:

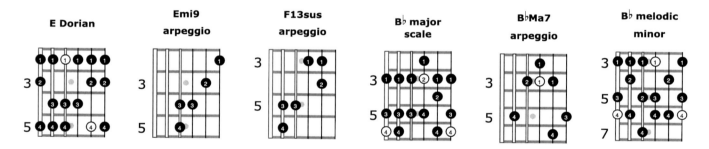

Example 113

Here there is more time to get into chord-scales, including the application of B♭ melodic minor on the E♭7♯11—the Lydian Dominant mode. On both the etude and improvisation I'm treating the F7 more as a C minor sound, giving it a suspended feeling. There is also time here for more chromaticism, which we find in the etude and improvisation. The etude and improvisation for the next position follow.

TRANE-TYPE CHANGES IMPROV #2

This position encompasses the 4th to 10th frets. Here are the shapes for the first four bars:

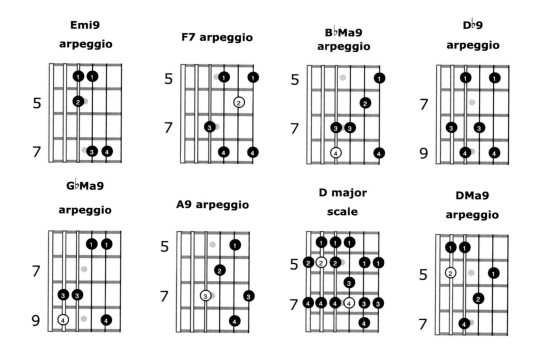

Example 114

More repetition of shapes: Example 114 is Example 111 transposed up a whole step, or two frets. In a progression with this many changes, and a harmonic sequence that repeats three times in three different keys, this repetition is inevitable. And it's a good thing too! **I find it easier to improvise when the material I am working with has some delimitation, especially on a tune this complex. Otherwise, there are too many choices.** Here are the shapes for the next four bars:

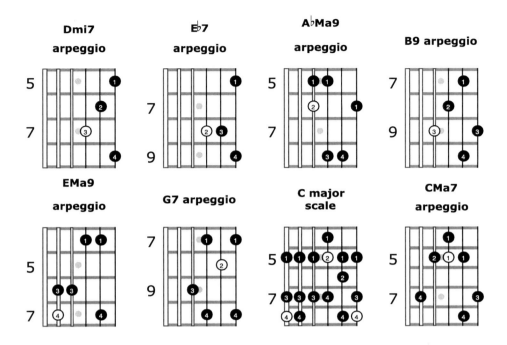

Example 115

There are many similarities with Example 112, but also some significant differences. The language I use in the etude and improvisation here is highly chromatic, and there is also significant anticipation of dominants, using the technique I explained in the text after Example 110 above. You can find such anticipations in measure 6 of the etude and in measure 5 of the improvisation. The next four bars' shapes:

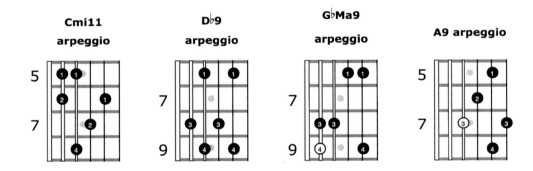

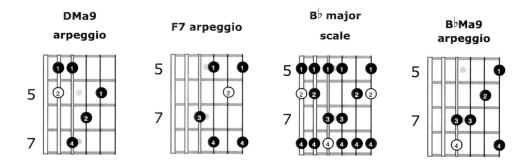

Example 116

As we learned in the previous position, many of the chords in bars 9-12 also occur in the bars 1-4, so there is repetition here. Unlike in previous chapters, I'm repeating the shapes, because the mind reels with all this modulation! As always, there is classic jazz chromaticism mixed in with arpeggios and scalar material. The final four bars use these shapes:

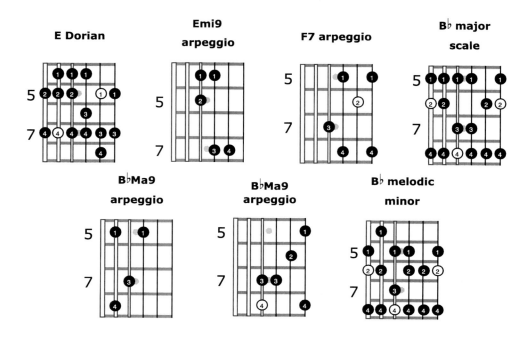

Example 117

These BbMa9 arpeggios could have been combined a la Example 24 from Chapter 2, and in the last measure of this Position 2 etude I use the Example 20 idea, also from Chapter 2, which hails from the melodic minor scale shape above. Take note of the chromaticism and the anticipations of the dominants. The etude and improvisation in the next position await your attention.

TRANE-TYPE CHANGES ETUDE #3

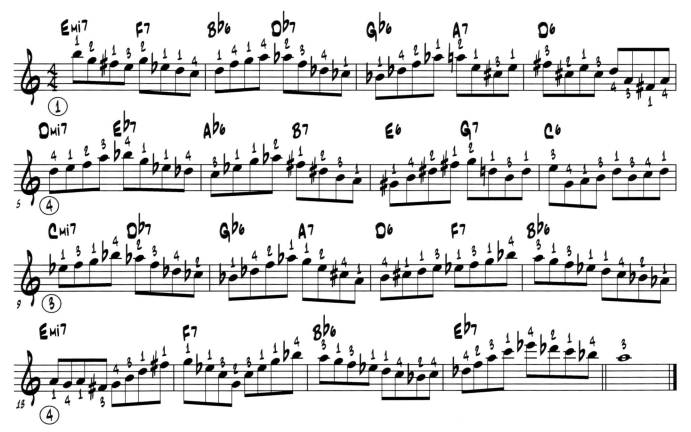

TRANE-TYPE CHANGES IMPROV #3

This position covers frets 6 to 11. Here are the shapes for the first four bars:

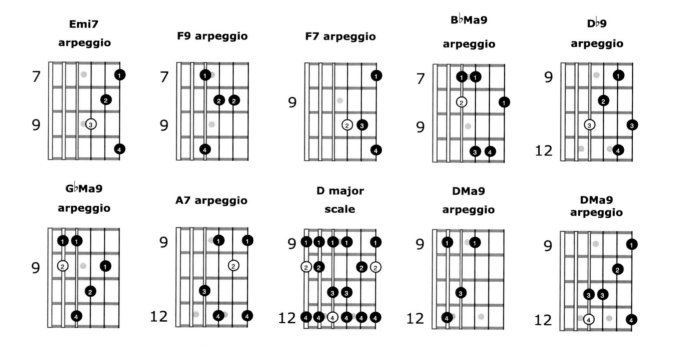

Example 118

We have seen these shapes before in previous positions, especially in Examples 112 and 115, which cover measures 9-12 in Position 1 and measures 5-8 in Position 2, respectively. There is an interesting anticipation of the A7 in measure 3 of the improvisation; the C♯ on the "and of 2," which is of course the major 3rd of A7, is also the perfect 5th of G♭6, enharmonically. **In my previous book, *Personalizing Jazz Vocabulary* (MB30786M), I refer to "negative guide tones," by which I mean notes that stay the same between chord changes, which can help your improvising sound smoother on tunes with complicated progressions like this one.** So in one sense the A7 is being anticipated here, while at the same time the C♯/D♭ is a sort of pivot note that connects the key area of G♭ major to the subsequent tonicization of D major. Here are the shapes for bars 5-9:

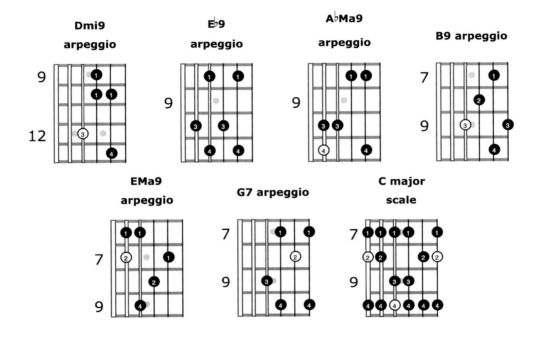

Example 119

These shapes are basically Example 116 transposed up a whole step, or two frets, although the Dmi9 arpeggio is a bit different. I'm straddling Position 3 and Position 4 on certain chords—on changes this complex and numerous I sometimes find myself in a sort of no-man's land, in between "grips." In the improvisation you can find the "negative guide tone" concept in effect on the "and of 2" G in measure 5 and the "and of 2" A♭ in measure 6. Those two pitches work on both chords, and help smooth the transition. Read on for the next four bars' shapes.

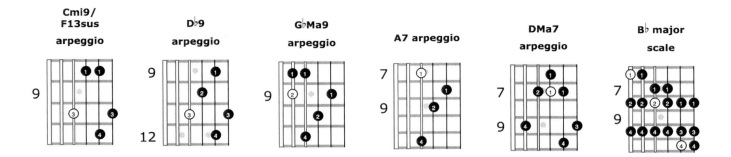

Example 120

Here we see some familiar shapes and some new ones, like the A7 arpeggio. This is a shape that I find rather awkward, one of those in-between grips that I usually avoid in favor of something a fret or two higher or lower. The F7 in measure 11 uses the same shape as the Cmi7 in measure 9. In the improvisation I actually get behind the chords a bit in measures 9 and 10. That used to happen to me quite often with this progression—less so since I've embraced the Barry Harris method of anticipating the dominants. Here are the shapes for the last four bars:

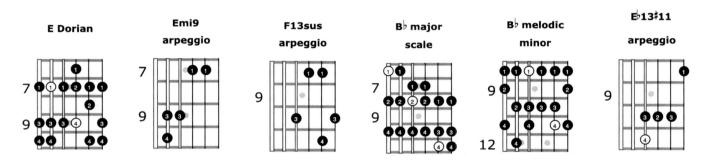

Example 121

The syncopation in the last four bars of the improvisation is an idea I associate with Jimmy Raney, especially the duets with his son Doug; the album *Nardis* is a personal favorite of mine. In the etude it is all scales and arpeggios, no chromaticism. Position 4 beckons.

Trane-type Changes Etude #4

105

TRANE-TYPE CHANGES IMPROV #4

This position covers frets 9 to 13. Here are the shapes for the first four bars:

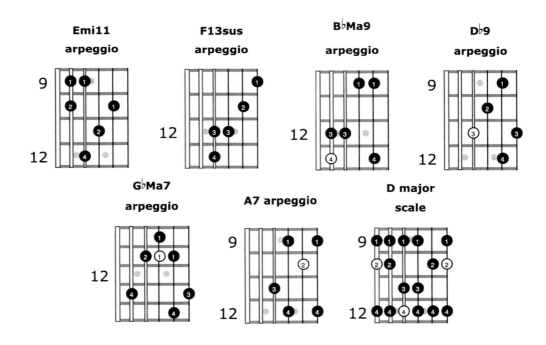

Example 122

106

We have seen all of these shapes before, particularly in Examples 116 and 119. In the etude on page 105, the F7 is treated more as a Cmi9 or F13sus, and the shape I use here is useful over minor sounds as well. **If this concept still seems unclear to you, now would be a good time to refer back to the chart in Example 6 from Chapter 1.** Both the etude and the improvisation contain idiomatic, classic jazz chromaticism, although none of the dominants are anticipated. Here are the shapes for the next four bars:

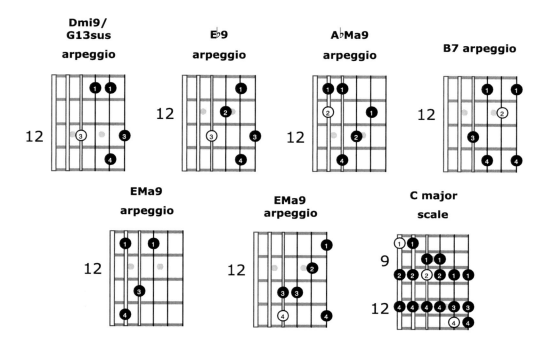

Example 123

I'm straddling two positions again, as in Example 119. **The ultimate point of playing in positions and learning these shapes is to be able to move freely up and down the length and width of the fretboard, so it isn't surprising that in the process of improvising and writing etudes I occasionally shift up or down slightly.** Measure 5 of the improvisation contains an anticipation of the E♭7. Here are the shapes for the next four bars:

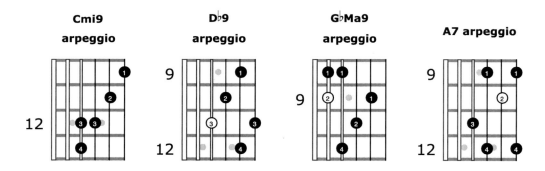

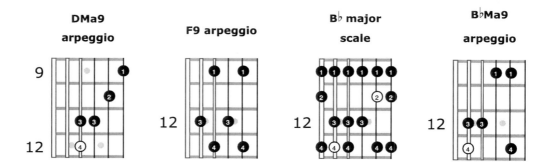

Example 124

The chords from the first four bars repeat, as do the shapes. The etude is all arpeggios and chord-scale material, whereas the improvisation has some classic jazz chromaticism, as per usual. Here are the shapes for the final four bars in this position:

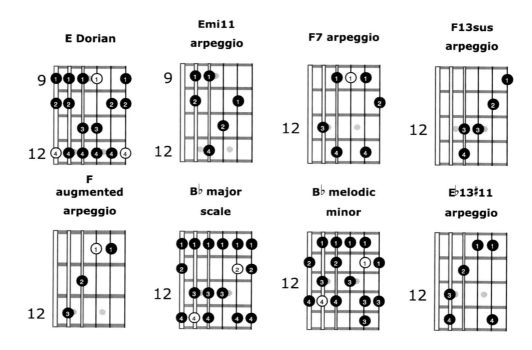

Example 125

The harmony in this progression moves so quickly that I rarely end up altering the dominants, but I managed to get an augmented triad into the F7-B♭6, V-I resolution in measure 14 of the etude. In fact, the material in this measure, along with the resolution on beat 1 of measure 15, makes a nice nine-eighth-note resolution cell. The rest of the material in this etude and improvisation consists of arpeggios, scale fragments, and chromaticism. Let's move on to the next position.

TRANE-TYPE CHANGES ETUDE #5

109

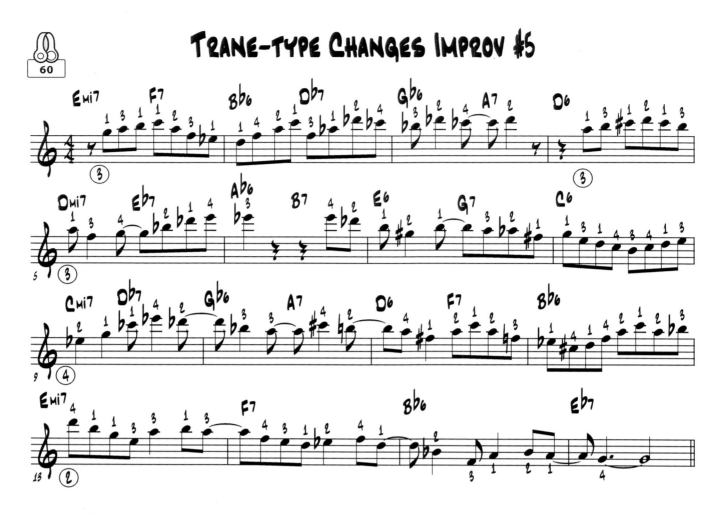

This position covers frets 11 to 17 or so. Here are the shapes for measures 1-4:

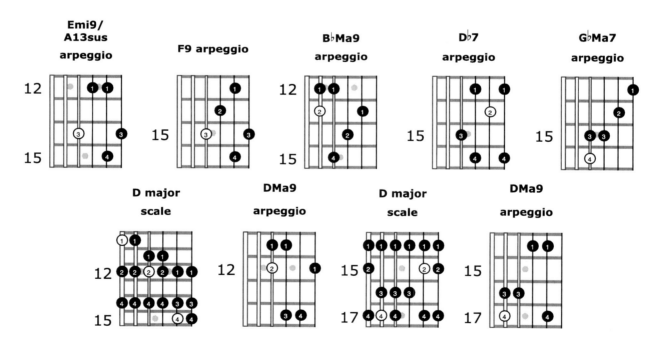

Example 126

These shapes are reminiscent of Examples 120 and 123. Again, there are only so many ways to arpeggiate major, minor, and dominant chords. Measure 4 uses different forms of the D major scale and arpeggio in the etude and improvisation. In fact, in the improvisation I jumped up to the next position—Position 1 in the higher octave. Otherwise, I'm just following the changes, with no anticipations or chromaticism this time. Here are the shapes for the next four measures:

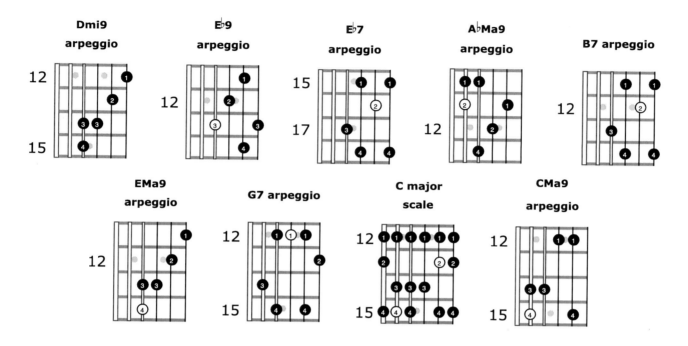

Example 127

I slipped up into the higher position again on the E♭7 during the improvisation, but then came back down. Otherwise, we have similar shapes to Example 124, and a dose of classic jazz chromaticism in the improvisation. Here are the next four bars' shapes:

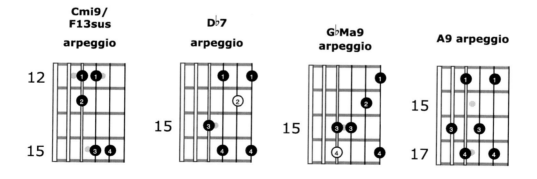

111

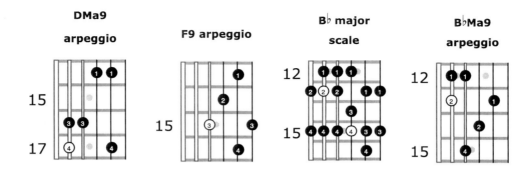

Example 128

These shapes hearken back to Examples 111 and 114. Same chords, same shapes—just a different chunk of the fretboard. In the improvisation there is some of the Raney-esque syncopation that I used back in Example 121, which causes the A7 to be anticipated by an 8th note. Both the etude and the improvisation have small doses of chromaticism as well. Here are the shapes for the final four bars:

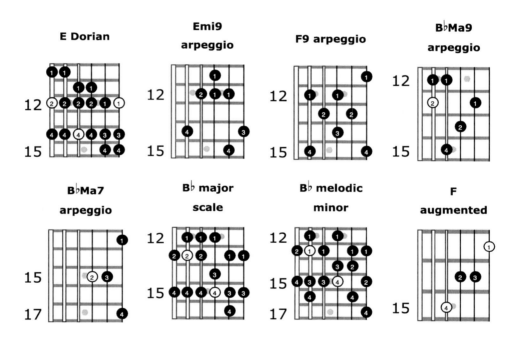

Example 129

As always with these last four bars, there is more time for scale material. There isn't any chromaticism here, but I outline an F augmented triad on the E♭7♯11 bar of the etude, which works because the upper-structure of E♭7♯11 contains such a triad.

This brings our exploration of these Trane-type changes to a close, and we have certainly covered the fretboard of the guitar thoroughly over these last five chapters. But what have we learned? Let us contemplate the labyrinth through which we have passed mostly unscathed.

CHAPTER 7

Out of the Labyrinth

In the previous five chapters we have covered a variety of modern jazz chord progressions, and explored their twists and turns through the analysis of the specific shapes that I use to improvise. This book represents the most exhaustive analysis of my own playing and process that I have undertaken. I hope that it will illuminate a path through the labyrinth of the guitar fretboard to you, dear reader, although I'm sure that some aspects of my journey will prove more helpful than others. As I stated in Chapter 1, I constructed my style and technique out of pieces of information borrowed from diverse sources, and it never felt systematic—rather, I took what I needed where I could get it, in the pre-internet era when information wasn't as easy to come by. I suggest you do the same with whatever resources are available to you.

The arpeggio and scale shapes that undergird these all-8th note etudes and improvisations are repetitive, but so too is improvising. I tell my students that I play the same things every time, just never in the same *order*, and never with the same phrase structure.

These days when I improvise, I close my eyes and the movements of my hands are automatic. I can hear what I'm going to play before I play it, but that's largely because I have played everything so many times: *I know what I sound like*. My fingers know where to go, but there are many things that can still go wrong, especially with these complicated modern-jazz structures. For example: issues of time, tempo, and feel, which this book says nothing about. But some days it all works out and I sound like myself, fully realized.

Like many people over the Covid-19 pandemic, I've been watching and playing a lot of online chess, and though my playing is, frankly, not very good, I see a useful analogy between what I do on the guitar and the knowledge of lines and openings and tactics that great chess players use to win their games. I definitely have an opening, middle, and end game in my improvisations. I have studied and memorized many great solos from past masters. But do I have an opponent? Perhaps not. Or maybe I'm playing both sides of the board...the analogy falls apart at some point, as all analogies must.

Still, the chess board with its ranks and files and pieces all moving their own way calls to mind the harmonic puzzles of modern jazz and the number of possible combinations and variations one can effectuate to "make the changes." Couple that with the mysteries of the labyrinth of the guitar fretboard: five places to play middle C, six (or seven) strings, twenty-plus frets, five fingers on each hand—so many ways to blunder. There are no checkmates or draws in our game, but it can be tempting to resign after a chorus or two.

All the labyrinths we human beings construct are daunting, but hopefully in this case if we work together and learn from each other we can navigate through and emerge with a deeper understanding of the mysteries of the music and the instrument, so we can make our art and express what we must.

About the Author

Davy Mooney

Davy Mooney is a jazz guitarist from New Orleans who records for Sunnyside Records and is Assistant Professor of Jazz Studies and head of the jazz guitar program at the University of North Texas, where he teaches private lessons and advanced jazz improvisation.

He has recorded seven CDs as a leader, and many others as a sideman. His latest Sunnyside CD, *Davy Mooney and the Hope of Home Band Live at National Sawdust*, was recorded live in Brooklyn, NY with Brian Blade, Jon Cowherd, John Ellis, and Matt Clohesy. In 2018 he recorded *Benign Strangers*, a collaboration with Japanese drummer Ko Omura (also on Sunnyside), and toured Japan to promote the release in the summer of 2018. His previous Sunnyside releases are 2017's *Hope of Home*, and 2012's *Perrier St*, both featuring Blade, Cowherd, Ellis, and Clohesy. In promotion of these CDs, Mooney has toured the US extensively, as well performed in Brazil, Japan, Mexico, Peru, and Myanmar.

Mooney's first book for Mel Bay, a guitar and improvisation instructional volume entitled *Personalizing Jazz Vocabulary*, was published in 2019.

Mooney has a PhD in jazz performance from New York University, and wrote a dissertation on the early 1960s work of Joe Pass entitled "Joe Pass's *Catch Me!*, *For Django*, and *Joy Spring*: Transcription and Analysis."

He competed in the 2005 Thelonious Monk International Guitar Competition, placing third, and studied at the Thelonious Monk Institute of Jazz Performance from 2007 to 2009, under artistic director Terence Blanchard. The Monk group worked with many jazz legends—including Herbie Hancock, Wayne Shorter, Dee Dee Bridgewater, and Ron Carter—and toured Panama and India.

Mooney received his Master's Degree from the University of New Orleans (his hometown) in 2005. Shortly thereafter (in the wake of Hurricane Katrina), he relocated to New York City, and began performing at clubs such as the 55 Bar, The Bar Next Door, The Blue Note, and Smalls. In 2006 he recorded a duo guitar CD with John Pizzarelli entitled *Last Train Home*. The following year he recorded *Astoriano*, released on the Japanese label LateSet Records.

Mooney has also made the foray into the literary world by self-publishing two novels: 2017's *Annalee* and 2012's *Hometown Heroes*.

For more info visit:
https://davymooney.bandcamp.com/album/live-at-national-sawdust
https://www.youtube.com/c/davymooneymusic
https://www.facebook.com/DavyMooneyMusic

Other Mel Bay Jazz Guitar Books

Jazz Warm-Ups for Guitar (Anthony)
Learning Tunes Workout (Cummiskey)
Mel Bay Jazz Guitar Curriculum: Diminished Workbook (Saunders)
Mel Bay Jazz Guitar Curriculum: Payin' Your Dues with the Blues (Umble)
Guitar Journals: Jazz (Multiple Authors)
Melodic Improvising for Guitar (Saunders)
Melodic Minor Guitar ...USC Curriculum (Pat Kelley)
Melodic Studies and Compositions for Guitar (Hamilton)
Modern Blues (Saunders)
Modern Jazz Guitar Styles (Bush)
Personalizing Jazz Vocabulary (Mooney)
Play-Along Jazz Standard Chords Progressions (Vignola)
Sight Reading for the Contemporary Guitarist (Bruner)
The Art of Picking (Jimmy Bruno)
The Changes (Sid Jacobs)
The Ultimate Map for Jazz Guitar (Anthony)
7-String Jazz Guitar Chord Chart (W. Bay)
21st Century Chords for Guitar (Bloom)
Achieving Guitar Artistry - Triads (W. Bay)
Basic Line Basics for Guitar (Chapman)
Coltrane Changes (C. Christiansen)
Comping the Blues (Vignola)
Complete Book of Harmony, Theory and Voicing (Willmott)
Complete Book of Harmonic Extensions for Guitar (Willmott)
Creative Comping Concepts for Jazz Guitar (Boling)
Deluxe Encyclopedia of Guitar Chords/Case Size (W. Bay)
Deluxe Encyclopedia of Guitar Chords/Full Size (W. Bay)
Deluxe Encyclopedia of Guitar Chord Progressions (Rector)
Drop 2 Concept for Guitar (Chapman)
George Van Eps Harmonic Mechanisms for Guitar Vol. 1
George Van Eps Harmonic Mechanisms for Guitar Vol. 2
George Van Eps Harmonic Mechanisms for Guitar Vol. 3
Guitar Fingerboard Harmony (McGuire)
Guitar Journals: Chords (W. Bay)
In the Pocket: Playing in the Groove (C. Christiansen)
Jazz Band Rhythm Guitar (Forman)
Jazz Guitar Chord Chart (W. Bay)
Jazz Guitar Chords Made Easy (W. Bay)
Jazz Gutar Essentials: Gig Savers Complete Edition (C. Christiansen)
Jazz Guitar Photo Chords (C. Christiansen)
Jazz Guitar Chord Substitution Wall Chart (C. Christiansen)
Jazz Guitar Chord Workout (C. Christiansen)
Jazz Guitar Comping (Andrew Green)
Jazz Chords for Rock Guitarists (Malone)
Joe Pass Guitar Chords
Modern Chords (Juris)

WWW.MELBAY.COM

WWW.MELBAY.COM